The Ethics of Climate Change

Think Now

Think Now is a new series of books which examines central contemporary social and political issues from a philosophical perspective. These books aim to be accessible, rather than overly technical, bringing philosophical rigour to modern questions which matter the most to us. Provocative yet engaging, the authors take a stand on political and cultural themes of interest to any intelligent reader.

The Ethics of Climate Change, James Garvey
Identity Crisis, Jeremy Stangroom
War and Ethics, Nicholas Fotion
Terrorism, Nicholas Fotion, Boris Kashnikov and Joanne K. Lekea

Series Editors:
James Garvey is Secretary of The Royal Institute of Philosophy and author of *The Twenty Greatest Philosophy Books* (Continuum)
Jeremy Stangroom is co-editor, with Julian Baggini, of *The Philosophers' Magazine* and co-author of *Why Truth Matters*, *What Philosophers Think* and *Great Thinkers A–Z* (all Continuum).

The Ethics of Climate Change

Right and Wrong in a Warming World

James Garvey

continuum

Continuum International Publishing Group
The Tower Building
11 York Road
London
SE1 7NX

80 Maiden Lane
Suite 704
New York
NY 10038

www.continuumbooks.com

First published 2008
Reprinted 2009

British Library Cataloguing-in-Publication Data
A catalogue record for this book is available from the British Library.

ISBN-10: HB: 0-8264-9738-1
        PB: 0-8264-9737-3
ISBN-13: HB: 978-0-8264-9738-3
        PB: 978-0-8264-9737-6

Library of Congress Cataloging-in-Publication Data
A catalog record for this book is available from the Library of Congress.

Typeset by Servis Filmsetting Ltd, Manchester
Printed and bound in the U.S.A. by Maple-Vail Book Manufacturing Group

Mixed Sources

Product group from well-managed forests, controlled sources and recycled wood or fibre

www.fsc.org   Cert no. SGS-COC-005368
© 1996 Forest Stewardship Council

FSC

30%

Contents

Introduction   **1**

Chapter 1: A Warmer World   **7**
  Strange changes   8
  Consensus   12
  Sound science   17
  Prospects   24

Chapter 2: Right and Wrong   **33**
  Philosophy and morality   34
  The importance of giving reasons   35
  Justifying moral beliefs   41
  Consistency, moral theories, intuitions   46
  Environmental ethics   49

Chapter 3: Responsibility   **57**
  Agency and spatial and temporal complexities   59
  The prisoner's dilemma and the tragedy of the
  commons   61
  Historical principles of justice   66
  Present entitlements and capacities   76
  Sustainability   83

Chapter 4: Doing Nothing   **89**
  Uncertainty   90
  Costs   97
  Technological rescue   101

	Waiting for others to act	106
	Urgency	110
Chapter 5:	**Doing Something**	**113**
	Criteria of moral adequacy	114
	UNFCCC and Kyoto	119
	Equal per capita shares	126
	Comparable burdens	130
Chapter 6:	**Individual Choices**	**137**
	Consistency again	138
	Psychological barriers	143
	Individual action	147
	Civil disobedience	151
Epilogue		**155**
Notes		**159**
Bibliography		**169**
Index		**175**

Introduction

It isn't easy to feel up to reflection on climate change. It can seem that you are unequal to it, and you can find yourself overwhelmed very quickly. Thinking about climate change is, partly, thinking about planetary upheaval, the deaths of countless living things, human suffering on an enormous scale, and all sorts of other horrors. It is possible to bracket your entirely normal and understandable reaction to all of that, put it off in a corner of your head and just get on with it. That's what I suggest you do if you find yourself feeling overwhelmed. It will pass. However, you'll need those normal reactions if you want to find your way through all of this to an honest, human conclusion or two. Your reactions are as important as fine-grained analysis. Anyway, I promise to keep as much of a lid on the horrors as I can.

The ethics of climate change is not all about the horrors. It has more to do with the fact that science alone cannot help us with the answers we need. The Intergovernmental Panel on Climate Change – and you will be hearing more about it in this book – has this to say about the role of science in our thinking about what to do about our warming world:

Natural, technical, and social sciences can provide essential information and evidence needed for decisions on what constitutes 'dangerous anthropogenic interference with the climate system'. At the same time, such decisions are value judgments determined through socio-political processes, taking into account considerations such as development, equity, and sustainability, as well as uncertainties and risk.[1]

Science can give us a grip on the facts, but we need more than that if we want to act on the basis of those facts. The something more which is needed involves values. Climatologists can tell us what is happening to the planet and why it is happening, they can even say with some confidence what will happen in the years to come. What we do about all of this, though, depends on what we think is right, what we value, what matters to us. You cannot find that sort of stuff in an ice core. You have to think your way through it.

This book is a start on those sorts of thoughts. It is not exhaustive or comprehensive, not the last word but a few first words. It is an introduction, in plain language, to the ethics of climate change, to where the moral weight falls on our changing planet and how that weight ought to translate into action. It has something to do with the conviction that our societies and our lives have to change, and the role of value in the changes ahead.

You might already wonder what 'value' means, exactly, in this context. Some people insist on definitions at the outset, but I'm with Socrates in thinking that definitions come at the end of an inquiry if they come at all, not the start. I'm happy for you to stick with whatever definition you like – at any rate, we'll narrow things down in Chapter 2. If I can get away with avoiding definitions for a while, probably I do owe you a short outline of the book. It might help you follow the arguments if you know what's coming. A philosophy book is no place for suspense.

This book begins with two chapters intended largely to shoo away distracting thoughts about the science of climate change and the nature of moral philosophy. The first chapter is about the settled scientific opinion on the climate of our warming world. I hope, by the end of it, that you will have some grip on the changes already underway, as well as the prospects for us and for the planet generally through the next hundred years or so. A large aim of the chapter is to put to one side the thought that there is uncertainty where it counts about climate change. A secondary aim is to be a little clearer about the prospects for human beings, in both the immediate and more distant future. The arguments to come depend at least a bit on the science of climate change.

The second chapter is about moral philosophy and, in particular, the nature of justifications for moral beliefs. Again, the main aim is to put some distractions to one side – for example, variations on the thought that we can never really justify our moral claims. I also hope, in a backhanded way, to give you a grip on at least a few moral theories which will figure in later arguments, as well as the approach to environmental ethics favoured in this book. Above all, I hope you come around to the conclusion that justifications for our moral beliefs matter, and the further conclusion that acting on the basis of those justifications matters too. Maybe it matters quite a bit.

Preliminaries aside, the third chapter takes up the nature of responsibility and climate change. We'll face up to several sorts of complexity, as well as a few troubles associated with collective rationality. We'll think about who should take action on climate change and come to some conclusions based on historical conceptions of justice, present entitlements and capacities, and sustainability.

Once we have some arguments on the table, arguments which amount to a moral demand for action on climate change, the fourth chapter will take up some pleas for inaction or minimal action. There might be other arguments for inaction, but the ones we'll consider seem to me to be the largest or anyway loudest. We'll find them all wanting in the end.

The fifth chapter is about action on climate change itself: what the world has done and what it should do. We'll identify several criteria which might be used to judge the moral adequacy of proposals for action, whatever they might be. We'll apply them to the United Nations Framework Convention on Climate Change, the Kyoto Protocol, and two different kinds of proposals for further or future action.

The final chapter narrows the focus from moral questions associated with global or governmental action on climate change to the moral status of individual choices, rights and wrongs in individual lives. There are some uncomfortable arguments to consider, and some conclusions to reach.

In the end, I suppose, I've left a lot of the reflection to you. Applied philosophy, as it is sometimes called, concerns itself with practical moral problems. Such things as abortion, euthanasia, genetic modification, healthcare, cloning and so on, raise philosophical questions which might be of interest to just about anyone. However, you can, all the while, be a little thankful that the problems are way over there, off at a safe distance. No one is about to clone you. With luck, you'll never be faced with problems having to do with abortion or euthanasia or the rest. However, you are lumped with the problem of climate change. It's a moral problem for you, right now. You have some decisions to make about how to live, some choices which concern your everyday life. There is some moral pressure on every one of us to come to some conclusions.

Some people who have helped me come to some conclusions, and others owed thanks for other sorts of help, are: Laura-May Abron, Quill Brogan, Tim Clark, Tom Crick, Crisis, Sarah Campbell, *Endeavour* and crew, Judy Garvey, Kim Hastilow, Ted Honderich, Joanna Kramer, Julia LeMense, Justin Lynas, Alex Mooney, Anthony O'Hear, associates at the Orwell, The Rock Ethics Institute, Ian Sillitoe, Barry Smith, Jeremy Stangroom, Joanna Taylor and UCLU Jitsu.

If you know the work of the growing number of philosophers who have devoted time to climate change – in particular, Stephen Gardiner, Dale Jamieson, Peter Singer and Henry Shue – you will recognize a number of other debts. If you don't know their work, take this book's bibliography to a library and get started. I have also relied, a lot, on the work of the IPCC, for which I am grateful.

This book is printed on paper from sustainable sources, in accord with the rules of the Forest Stewardship Council. A portion of the royalties due both to the publisher and to me have been donated to green charities. I'm glad to be associated with a publisher like Continuum.

Finally, this book is dedicated to Yolonne MacKenzie, with thanks for help with my shoelaces.

1   A Warmer World

The rays from the sun and fixed stars could reach the earth through the atmosphere more easily than the rays emanating from the earth could get back into space.

John Tyndall

This chapter deals with the scientific preliminaries to a consideration of the moral dimension of climate change. We can zero in on ethics once we're as clear as we can be about the facts. Two misconceptions must be dealt with at the outset. First, if you are not there already, then I hope to bring you around to believing that climate change is not some distant prospect which won't affect us in our lifetimes. It is, in fact, already well underway. In the second section, we will look briefly at the scientific consensus with respect to the existence of anthropogenic climate change and put to one side the otherwise distracting notion that there is a climate change debate in the scientific community or that there is some troubling level of scientific uncertainty about the basic facts of climate change. It will help to know a little something about the science underpinning all of this, and we will deal with that in the third section. In the final section, we will take up some predictions about the future of our climate and planet. Even if you accept that the climate is changing and know more or less how and why it is occurring, some of the larger moral problems won't really bite unless you know something about our prospects, the prospects for us as a species, in the face of climate change. Those prospects are not rosy.

STRANGE CHANGES

It is sometimes thought that climate change is remote, a problem for our children but not us. In fact, our world is already getting warmer. In terms of global average near-surface temperatures, the 1980s and 1990s were the warmest decades since accurate records began in the mid to late 1800s.[1] Eleven of the last twelve years are among the warmest years on the instrumental record. The first decade of this unpleasant millennium is shaping up to top even the 1990s. Globally averaged surface temperatures have increased by about 0.7 degrees Celsius over the twentieth century, with the hottest years on average coming later and later.[2] An increase of 0.7 degrees might not impress you, but it impresses climatologists who know that the speed of the change is without precedent over at least the past 10,000 years. Notice also that this is an average increase – some places on the planet, particularly land masses, are getting considerably warmer. It's worth pausing for a moment and thinking about the nature of this warmer world we now inhabit and the effects of just this apparently teeny average increase of 0.7 degrees.

The average sea level has risen by an annual rate of nearly 2 mm since 1960, with the rate increasing to about 3 mm per year between 1993 and 2003. The general increase is partly due to thermal expansion – water takes up more space when it gets warmer – as well as run-off from melting glaciers and losses from the ice sheets of Greenland and Antarctica. It might not seem like much of an increase to you, but if you think about the vastness of the Earth's oceans, and the volume of water required to make a noticeable dent in them, it's actually an enormous change.

This is a fact not lost on any of the one thousand or so people who live on the Carteret Islands in the South Pacific. The highest land they've got is only just above sea level, and the tides have been rising lately, inundating homes, destroying food and potable water supplies. In 2005, Papua New Guinea put aside funds for the total evacuation of the island, ten families at a time, by the year 2007. This is cutting it a little close: it's likely that the islands will be entirely submerged by 2015. All of this is being watched with interest by the 12,000 inhabitants of the low-lying island nation of Tuvalu. There, sea water is bubbling up through the ground, and seasonal flooding is becoming more and more dramatic. People have lived on Tuvalu for more than 2,000 years, but they are talking now of abandoning the place, perhaps starting over in New Zealand. You can stare out of a window for a while, wondering what it would be like to know that your hometown, your homeland, is simply gone.

The people of the Carteret Islands and Tuvalu are among the first to be called 'climate refugees' or 'environmental refugees'. They won't be the last. Their stories seem to have been seized upon by the press, but according to some estimates they are certainly not alone in being displaced by our changing climate. We haven't settled on a clear way of defining a climate refugee, and statistics are all over the place. The Red Cross argue that there were about 25 million environmental refugees as of 2001.[3] That's larger than the figure they give for the number of people who have been displaced by wars. No doubt the number, whatever it really is, is growing.

A warmer world is also a melting world. The amount of time that the rivers and lakes of the northern hemisphere are covered in ice has decreased by about two weeks in the last century. Further north, and more dramatically, Arctic sea-ice has thinned by 40 per cent in the summers of the most recent decades, compared to their thickness at the start of the twentieth century. It has also simply melted away: anywhere from 10–15 per cent of sea-ice is just gone. Average Arctic temperatures have increased at nearly two times the global average rate over the past 100 years. Non-polar glaciers are also in widespread retreat. We can now see, from satellite images, that the parts of our planet which are covered in snow each winter have decreased by as much as 10 per cent. That's an observation made in recent decades, just since we've been able to look down from above, since we stuck some satellites in space and started to take an interest. All of this has had disturbing effects on the plants and animals whose lives are somehow tied to the ice and snow. Polar bears, for example, need the sea-ice for hunting seals. That ice is now disappearing. I'm not sure what to make of it, but for possibly the first time, polar bears have begun to eat each other.[4]

One of the most worrying aspects of the melt – in addition to the increased risk of flood for coastal places, changes to plant and animal life, and the loss of drinking water from glacial run-off – is what's happening to permafrost. 'Permafrost', it turns out, is not an apt name. It consists in complicated layers of ground which stay more or less frozen all year round. Some of it has spent hundreds of thousands of years taking the shape it now has, and it is melting, from the top down, nearly everywhere. Temperatures at the top of the permafrost layer have increased by as much as 3 degrees since the 1980s. This is worrying for lots of reasons, but perhaps the largest one has to do with carbon. Permafrost has a lot of dead stuff in it, dead animal and plant matter, and that dead stuff has carbon in it. Because permafrost is normally frozen, bacteria cannot get to work on it, so the carbon stays put. If it starts to melt, a huge amount of carbon – maybe as much as 450 billion metric tons – will find its way into the atmosphere, accelerating the planet's warming. This is one of those positive planetary feedback mechanisms you might have heard about. We'll come round to them in due course.

The changes to our planet are not just happening somewhere distant, like the poles or the tundra. El Niño affects the weather around the world. Roughly every three to five years, the sea and atmosphere in and around the centre of the Pacific Ocean undergo a change. In particular, El Niño conditions are associated with warmer than usual surface temperatures at sea, which affect the temperature of the atmosphere, ocean currents and, in general, weather throughout the globe. For example, El Niño conditions lead to warmer and wetter weather in South America and considerably drier weather in Southeast Asia and Australia. During particularly intense El Niño years, South America is subject to violent storms and severe flooding, and parts of Australia experience crushing droughts and widespread bush fires. The effects do not just happen on land. Coral reefs tend to bleach during El Niño events – the symbiotic algae living within them are expelled due to heat stress and the structures turn a chalky white. Many corals are very slow to recover, if recover they do. Almost all of the coral in large parts of the Indian Ocean now makes up a dead, bleached, brittle coral graveyard.

The warming of the Earth has resulted in more frequent, persistent and intense El Niño events during the past 20 to 30 years as compared to the last 100 years, and the floods and droughts associated with these events have followed suit in both intensity and frequency. One way to think about this is to reflect on the damage caused by extreme weather. There's nothing like a gauge for this sort of thing, but there certainly is a record of weather-related economic losses. Adjusted for inflation, global losses rose an entire order of magnitude in just the last 40 years. Insurance companies have changed the way they do business. Try not to let yourself get too immersed in the numbers. Catastrophic weather events result in something more than economic losses: the loss of human life. The part of that loss which is tied to El Niño events has been increasing lately too.

Planetary changes are not just affecting human beings. Plant and animal ranges have moved towards the poles or into higher and cooler ground. Insects are emerging earlier, birds are migrating earlier, plants are blooming earlier, breeding seasons arrive earlier and last longer. Some plants and animals are adapting to the changes, but others, particularly those already threatened by other factors, are unable to change. The speed of change is just too much for many creatures. Migration will work for some animals, but others just lack the option. A mountain gorilla which needs cooler weather will move up the mountain to find it. Until it runs out of mountain. Whole species have already died out as a result of climate change.

An increase of 0.7 degrees is doing something to our planet right now – to its ice and snow and permafrost, its oceans, its weather patterns, its land, and its plants and animals, including us. There are good reasons to think that the pace of the warming is increasing. We'll come to those reasons in due course, but for now, just think a little about the predicted temperature changes, changes which will no doubt shape the future of our warming world.

In 2000, a number of predictions were made.[5] For the period between 1990 and 2025, the projected increase was thought to be between 0.4 and 1.1 degrees – at minimum, this meant that there would be more than half as much warming in 35 years as in the past 100 years. For the period between 1990 and 2050, the projected increases were between 0.8 and 2.6 degrees. By the end of the present century, the projected increases were between 1.4 to 5.8 degrees in total, two to ten times more warming than that observed over the whole of the twentieth century.

Those predicted ranges, unnerving enough, were revised upwards at the top end in 2007. By 2100, current estimates for temperature increase range between 1.1 and 6.4 degrees. There has not been an increase of this magnitude for at least the past 10,000 years. Those who know how to read the bubbles of ancient air trapped in ice cores have concluded that the planet has not warmed so suddenly for at least 400,000 years, if ever.

As we have seen, an increase of 0.7 degrees is already doing something to our planet but have a think about the next 15 or 50 or 100 years. What will happen when global average temperatures rise by anything between 1 and 7 degrees? It will happen. We are already committed to it.

CONSENSUS

You might have heard something about scientific uncertainty concerning climate change or the so-called 'climate change debate'.

The debate has had a hearing and sometimes still gets one – books, documentaries, talk shows and even honest newspapers go in for it from time to time. It has been given time on the floor of the US Senate. Senator James Inhofe, for example, expressed the Bush administration's party line at the time by saying, 'The claim that global warming is caused by man-made emissions is simply untrue and not based on sound science.'[6]

There is, though, nothing like a debate among scientists when it comes to either the fact of climate change or the human role in it. A very few people outside of the scientific community or somewhere on its fringes actually do say that the climate is not changing. Others accept the fact of change but insist that it is part of a natural variation, not at all caused by human beings. Some wallow in the absurdity that warmer temperatures will benefit the human race. Much has been made of the connection between the fossil-fuel industry and climate-change scepticism, but we will look away from that here.

There is, just as a matter of fact, a remarkable scientific consensus about the existence of anthropogenic or human-induced climate change. We'll glance at it in a moment for one reason. The mistaken view that there is no consensus in the scientific community needs to die a death. This view is taken seriously in some quarters – even some quarters that matter, like the US Senate – and it shouldn't be. It gets in the way of our real focus, the ethical demands associated with climate change. It won't detain us for long.

What follows, let me emphasize, is not an appeal to authority. Appeals to authority are rightly considered fallacious because the truth of a claim can never be established by the fact that someone authoritative said it. We've known about the fallacy for a long time. Followers of Pythagoras tried to justify their assertions by saying, roughly, 'Pythagoras *himself* said it'. Maybe they stomped their feet a little. The Ancient Greeks didn't fall for it, and neither do we, usually. The mistake is easiest to spot when the expert holding forth is not an expert on the matter under consideration. Actors know lots of truths about props and costumes, but their expertise does not extend to politics. Even if they happen to be right, the fact that they say that the war is wrong is not a good reason for thinking that the war is wrong.

Matters are complicated if you notice that even when an expert holds forth on a topic well within his area of expertise, the fact that he is the one holding forth cannot settle the truth of what he says. Experts can get things wrong or have ulterior motives. Still, we are not trying to settle the truth of anything over and above the existence of a scientific consensus concerning climate change, and in this context, what the experts say matters more than anything. It turns out that almost all the authorities agree on quite a bit, certainly on the fact that the climate is warming and that human beings are a cause of it. The following is a bare-bones account of the history of that consensus.

In 1988, two UN bodies, the World Meteorological Organization and the United Nations Environment Programme, were collectively worried about the possibility of climate change. They established the Intergovernmental Panel on Climate Change (IPCC), which was and still is charged with assessing the scientific evidence for climate change by examining peer-reviewed, technical literature. The IPCC also aims to offer information and advice to policy makers and others concerned with changes to the climate. Three working groups make up the IPCC – one deals with the physical basis of climate change, another with the various possible or likely impacts of climate change, and a third with mitigation strategies. The IPCC is also home to a task force which inventories greenhouse-gas emissions.

The entire body is staffed by hundreds of experts from all over the world, and its work has been called the largest international scientific undertaking in human history, probably rightly so. Its efforts come together in several books and, perhaps most importantly, assessment reports published at intervals of roughly five years. The reports are taken by virtually everyone working on climate change as authoritative. Most see the reports and publications of the IPCC as evidence of a growing scientific consensus on various aspects of the climate.

Over the years, the language in the reports has grown stronger and stronger, reflecting the growing confidence of the scientific community. Slightly tentative, early claims have been replaced by stronger talk grounded in a better understanding of the climate and the mechanisms of change. The first report, which appeared in 1990, acknowledged uncertainties about the speed and magnitude of climate change, as well as the role of human action in it. The fact of change, though, was never in doubt. Even as early as its first report, the IPCC urged all countries to take immediate action to reduce the impact of impending changes to the climate. The second report, issued in 1995, made more specific predictions about the pace and nature of climate change, as well as the further claim that a 'balance of the evidence showed a discernable human influence on climate'. By 2001 and the publication of the third report, the IPCC was even more confident: 'There is new and stronger evidence that most of the warming observed over the last 50 years is attributable to human activities.' Ranges of effects and the pace of change, based on different models of the climate, were pressed home in detail. The fourth and most recent report, published in 2007, leaves no room at all for doubt: 'Warming of the climate system is unequivocal, as is now evident from observations of increases in global average air and ocean temperatures, widespread melting of snow and ice, and rising global average sea level.'

Other bodies have offered statements in support of the findings of the IPCC. The National Academy of Sciences has over 2,000 of America's best brains on the books, including 200 Nobel Prize winners. In a report on climate change published in 2001, the Academy found that the IPCC's work was a fair and accurate summary of current climate science. Its own views on climate change are straightforward: 'Greenhouse gases are accumulating in the Earth's atmosphere as a result of human activities, causing surface air temperatures and subsurface ocean temperatures to rise.'[7]

The National Academy is not the only US scientific body to support the findings of the IPCC. In 2003, the American Meteorological Society concluded that there 'is now clear evidence that the mean annual temperature at the Earth's surface, averaged over the entire globe, has been increasing in the past 200 years. . . . Human activities have become a major source of environmental change . . .'[8] In the same year, the American Geophysical Union adopted a statement which claims that scientific evidence strongly indicates both that the climate of the planet is changing and that human activities are partly responsible for the changes.[9] The US Climate Change Science Program, which undertakes research on behalf of 13 federal agencies in the US, published a report in 2006 which expanded on the science underpinning the findings of the IPCC. The report argues that the observed patterns of climate change over the past 50 years cannot be explained by natural factors alone – the human production of greenhouse gasses is responsible as well.[10]

Scientific opinion outside of the US is firmly behind the IPCC too. In June 2005, just ahead of the G8 summit, the national science academies of Canada, France, Germany, Italy, Japan, Russia, the UK, Brazil, China and India signed a statement in support of the findings of the IPCC. The statement claims that 'there is now strong evidence that significant global warming is occurring. . . . It is likely that most of the warming can be attributed to human activities.'[11] The statement goes on to urge nations to take steps to limit carbon emissions and take swift action to adapt to the impending effects of climate change.

Following a campaign undertaken by the Royal Society in the UK, the national or regional scientific academies of Australia, Belgium, Brazil, Canada, the Caribbean, China, France, Germany, India, Indonesia, Ireland, Italy, Malaysia, New Zealand and Sweden issued a joint statement on the science of climate change in 2001. It's difficult to misinterpret the paper: 'The work of the Intergovernmental Panel on Climate Change represents the consensus of the international scientific community on climate change science.

We recognize the IPCC as the world's most reliable source of information on climate change and its causes'.[12]

In short, there is a lot of agreement among experts all over the world about both the changing climate and our role in it.[13] If you had some doubts, maybe thought that scientific reflection on climate change had not yet got past the question of whether or not it is real and occurring, then hopefully those doubts are behind you. Understanding the actual mechanisms of climate change should help you get your hooks into the moral debate, and we'll now turn, briefly, to the science of climate change.

SOUND SCIENCE

The science underpinning our understanding of the effects of carbon dioxide and other gases on the temperature of the planet is not at all new.[14] The warming effect of atmospheric gases was first noticed by Jean-Baptiste Fourier in 1827. He was also the first to make a comparison between the effects of such gases and the glass of a greenhouse or hothouse, and the name 'greenhouse gases' stuck. What interested Fourier and others at the time was not the nature of a warming world, but how ice ages were possible – how, in other words, a comfy world like ours could turn into a frozen one and somehow back again. It was clear that large parts of the planet had been covered in huge sheets of ice in the past. What no one understood were the mechanisms responsible for such dramatic climactic changes. How could everything just freeze up like that?

It was John Tyndall who argued that a cause of the ice ages might be a decrease in atmospheric carbon dioxide and, thus, a diminishing of the greenhouse effect. With characteristic flair, he writes:

> The solar heat possesses the power of crossing an atmosphere, but when the heat is absorbed by the planet, it is so changed in quality that

the rays emanating from the planet cannot get with the same freedom back into space. Thus, the atmosphere admits of the entrance of the solar heat but checks its exit; the result is a tendency to accumulate heat at the surface of this planet.[15]

He was the first to offer experimental proof of all of this by measuring the absorption of heat by carbon dioxide, water vapour and other gases.

Still concerned with explaining the climactic shifts responsible for ice ages, the Swedish chemist Svante Arrhenius carried out a series of calculations which showed that decreasing the amount of atmospheric carbon dioxide by half would lower average surface temperatures by four to five degrees. His colleague Arvid Högbom was interested in the ways in which carbon was put into and removed from the atmosphere by natural processes – like the output of carbon by volcanoes and the absorption of it by oceans. Arrhenius drafted him in to help explain ice ages. Högbom was the first to take seriously the possibility that burning fossil fuels and, thus, producing greenhouse gases could raise the planet's average temperature. Arrhenius took an interest in this too, and in 1896 he did the calculations, finding that a doubling in the amount of carbon dioxide in the atmosphere would increase global average temperatures by five to six degrees. His calculations might not be far off.

However, no one saw this as cause for alarm or as even slightly worrying. Given the levels of carbon dioxide produced at the end of the nineteenth century, it was thought that several thousand years would be needed to double the carbon concentration in the atmosphere. No one at the time banked on the huge increase in planetary population and fuel consumption which would characterize the next century. At any rate, no one doubted for a moment that the vast oceans would absorb most of the carbon and largely counteract our industrial output.

Just over 50 years later, though, the amateur meteorologist G. S. Callendar correlated documented increases in atmospheric carbon and increases in average temperature. In 1957, Hans Suess and Roger Revelle found that the oceans were not absorbing carbon at anything like the rate which had previously been assumed. They argued that 'human beings are now carrying out a large scale geophysical experiment of a kind that could not have happened in the past nor be reproduced in the future'.[16]

It was the first loud warning about climate change, the first serious expression of concern from the scientific community.

This thumbnail sketch alone should tell you that lots of things are taken as just true and uncontroversial by climate scientists. The fact that the Sun heats the Earth is a hard one to miss. We have known at least since Tyndall that various gases present in the atmosphere absorb some of that heat as it radiates back from the Earth, stopped short on its way into space. We have noticed since Arrhenius and Högbom that burning fossil fuels puts some of these gases in the atmosphere and that putting enough of them up there will increase surface temperatures. We've known since Suess and Revelle that we are doing just that, namely, putting a lot of carbon in the atmosphere and probably changing the temperature of the planet. All of this has taken a while to sink in – there have been objections and arguments, as well as experiments and head scratching – but it's now just data, and the data are by no means thumbnail in detail.

Probably the easiest way to think about the details, in particular the easiest way to get a grip on the greenhouse effect, is to think of the Earth's atmosphere as a kind of blanket. This image appears in almost all low-brow descriptions of the workings of our climate which I manage to understand. The radiation emitted by the Sun passes through the atmosphere more or less unimpeded and gets absorbed by the stuff on the surface of the planet. The stuff, depending on what sort of stuff it is, emits various amounts of thermal radiation. Some of the gases present in the atmosphere absorb this radiation and thus keep some warmth in the atmosphere which would otherwise leach out into space.

Quite a few gases, most notably water vapour, do this entirely naturally, and the so-called 'natural greenhouse effect' is by all accounts a good thing. Without it, the planet would have average temperatures a bit below freezing. Other gases, like carbon dioxide, methane and nitrous oxide, occur naturally too and contribute to the natural greenhouse effect. The trouble is that these other gases are also among the by-products of burning fossil fuels and other human activities having to do with our use of the land. We have been adding them to the atmosphere and so enhancing the natural greenhouse effect. Carbon dioxide tends to be the focus here, because it is responsible for around 70 per cent of the enhanced or anthropogenic greenhouse effect. Methane, though, is no slouch: although we put less of it in the atmosphere, a molecule of methane causes about eight times the greenhouse effect as caused by a molecule of carbon dioxide. Once in the atmosphere, these gases act as a blanket, keeping in some of the heat. By burning fossil fuels and putting more greenhouse gases in the atmosphere, we are, in effect, thickening the blanket, and that thickening is warming the planet.

How much carbon have we added to the atmosphere? The amount of carbon in the atmosphere varies quite a lot if you are interested in long time frames, if you look back over hundreds of thousands or millions of years. However, for several thousand years before we began to burn fossil fuels in earnest, before the Industrial Revolution got underway around 1750, the amount of carbon in the atmosphere hovered near 280 parts per million. During this fairly long stretch of relative stability, human beings went from scruffy bands of hunter-gatherers to well-dressed, well-spoken, civilized modern human beings, with cities and culture and reservations for dinner. It is possible to think that there is a connection between that period of climactic stability and the rise of human civilization. It's also possible to worry that this period of stability is coming to an end.

Since the start of the Industrial Revolution, human beings have dumped an astonishing 600,000 million tons (or gigatons) of carbon dioxide into the atmosphere. The concentration floating around up there has increased by nearly 30 per cent since the

Industrial Revolution, and it's now 370 parts per million. Presently, we add another 6 or 7 gigatons each year. The amount pumped into the atmosphere is, and has been, increasing annually. In a very short period of time, we have changed the composition of our atmosphere rather dramatically. Not only are we still adding to the amount of carbon in the atmosphere, but it is also true that it takes a while for the planet's oceans, plants and creatures to drag some of it back out of the air. If the machine ground to a halt tomorrow and not a whisper of carbon made it into the atmosphere as a result of human activities, we would still be lumbered with some level of enhanced greenhouse effect for hundreds if not thousands of years.

One question which might occur to you, if you are naturally inclined to scepticism, is, well, how do we know that it's us? Maybe we can measure the amount of carbon up there right now, and probably we can work out how much was there before the Industrial Revolution by examining ice cores, sediments, tree rings and such. Maybe, too, the science connecting carbon dioxide to warming is well established. Despite all this, there can remain a sliver of doubt. How do we know that it's the greenhouse gases we put into the atmosphere that's doing the damage, that's causing the changes? Couldn't it be some other factor, maybe natural variation or sunspots or a cause or causes as yet unidentified? For that matter, how do we know about predicted increases in temperatures, mentioned at the start of this chapter, which are as far off as the end of this century?

The answers to these questions have everything to do with climate models, and climate models are unspeakably complicated things. You can ease yourself into thinking about them, a little, by considering something comparatively simpler but complex enough: a one-day computer weather forecast.

The Met Office in the UK is obviously in the business of producing regular weather forecasts, and it accomplishes this, in part, by being connected up to a worldwide weather network called the Global Telecommunications System. This enormous planetary web of computers automatically blips out a huge amount of information to and from stations all over the globe. Data concerning everything you might want to know about temperature, pressure, wind speed, precipitation and on and on are gathered from such varied sources as satellites, ships, radar stations, remote buoys, manned and unmanned ground stations, oil rigs, balloons and so on. The entire planet is peppered with monitoring stations.

All of this information is fed automatically to places like the Met Office, which loads the lot into a supercomputer. The computer then does a considerable amount of number crunching, working at speed through mathematical equations which describe the physical processes governing the way the weather develops. From the initial conditions supplied by the global system, through the mathematics, you get a forecast based on a mathematical representation of how the system will be doing tomorrow.

A climate model works much like this, but climate models have to take account of more complex aspects of the planet which do not matter much in the short term. It nearly goes without saying that climate models are much more forward-looking than weather forecasts. Instead of operating with a snapshot of the planet's weather, a climate model is concerned with longer periods of time: from a few years to many decades. Climate models produce information about averages of certain aspects of the weather (like temperature, pressure, precipitation, etc.) as well as statistical variations from those averages, over long periods of time. The number crunching undertaken by a supercomputer running a climate model involves not just mathematical representations of the sorts of physical processes found on a weather model, but various feedbacks in the climate system and other sorts of linkages which might take some time to play out, as well as further factors which matter over longer periods.

For instance, the atmosphere, oceans, land, ice and the plants and animals of our world have large effects on each other over time, and these effects can have a bearing on the nature of the climate. Some of these interconnections, though, manifest themselves as feedbacks in the climate system, and they can make a massive difference to what the model predicts. To give you a cartoonish example, if the atmosphere becomes warmer on average, then more water will evaporate from the oceans and rivers. This means that a warmer atmosphere will have more water vapour in it than a cooler one. Since water vapour has a substantial greenhouse effect, a positive feedback results: a warmer atmosphere is a wetter atmosphere, and a wetter atmosphere will get still warmer over time.

How do we know that these models are accurate? The obvious answer is the right one: you set the model to run with information from five or five thousand years ago and see how its predications square with what you already know about the past climate. You can also double-check a model by seeing how it responds to unusual events which result in climate anomalies. If you already know that a particular volcanic eruption resulted in all sorts of local and even planetary changes, and you have detailed records of all of this, you can pop the eruption into your model and see how it squares with what you know actually happened. The details you are comparing can be extraordinarily fine-grained.

I've made all of this sound less complex than it is. Some climate models which run 100 years into the future can involve over a quadrillion different operations and take more than a month to complete. There are lots of climate centres all over the world running different climate models, and there are as many as hundreds of people employed at each centre, each one probably working on some extraordinarily specific aspect of the model or the algorithms or the data or our world. These people are getting better and better at what they do, and the models are becoming more and more accurate. The models can be very persuasive.

One of the most visually impressive results of climate modelling was reproduced by the IPCC in 2001. The report contains a series of three graphs which compare annual global mean surface temperatures as simulated by models and as actually observed from 1860 to 2000. In the first graph only natural forces with a bearing on temperature were factored into the model. There is not much of a match between observed and modelled temperatures here. In the second, only anthropogenic greenhouse gases were used in the model's calculation, and the result is a closer match to observed temperatures. The third model's results, which best match observed temperatures, take into account natural and human factors.

The most recent report of the IPCC takes account of not just models, but what it now calls 'direct observations of climate change'. Scientists, traditionally cautious creatures, are now willing to say that we can see it happening. Whether you buy into the models or not, it is hard to escape the conclusion that human beings have had an effect on the climate, probably a substantial effect. It can lead you to wonder about the effects we will have on the climate of the future.

PROSPECTS

What can be said about the future of our warming planet?[17] The changes we have set in motion, the changes outlined in the first section of this chapter, are going to carry on for a while no matter what we do. The planet will certainly become warmer. Among other things, we are not sure just how much carbon dioxide we will put into the atmosphere in the future or just what the planet's feedback mechanisms might do. So there is some uncertainty in the magnitude and timing and also the regional variability of our estimates. Nevertheless, we know that we are committed to an increase in globally averaged surface temperature of 1.1 to 6.4 degrees during this century. According to the reports of paleoclimatologists, this increase is unprecedented during at least the past 10,000 years – some argue that the planet has not been as warm for at least 400,000 years.

You can think of the speed and enormity of the change ahead by thinking about ice ages and the temperate, interglacial periods which bookend them. The difference in temperatures between ice ages and warmer periods is about 5 or 6 degrees. By human as opposed to geological standards, it takes a very long time for the planet to shift itself from an ice age to a relatively warm period. The temperature changes ahead of us in just the current century are anywhere from a third to an entire ice age's worth of change. The change is astonishingly rapid by planetary standards. Further, we are heading in an odd direction. The world is moving towards the opposite of an ice age, whatever that might be.

Note that the temperatures mentioned are global averages. Some places will have increases of much more than 1.1 to 6.4 degrees on average – land masses as opposed to ocean surfaces, and particularly polar and tropical regions. There will be higher maximum temperatures, more hot days, and more heat waves all over the planet. Conversely, there will be higher minimum temperatures, and fewer cold days or frosts. This general increase will exacerbate the effects which have already been noticed, the changes our world is already undergoing.

For example, the future will be characterized by more extreme weather events. As our planet gets warmer, evaporation will increase, more water vapour will find its way into the air, and some parts of the world will experience much more or much less precipitation. It's not going to be an even spread of extra rain. Climatologists say that the Earth's hydrological cycle will become more intense, and by this they mean more extreme weather events will occur – extremes in both directions, both wet and dry. The frequency and intensity of heavy showers, thunderstorms and flooding will increase in some places, as will the frequency of landslides, avalanches and mudslides. In other areas, the frequency and intensity of droughts or general drops in levels of precipitation will increase. In such places, crops will be damaged or fail to grow, water for both agriculture and human consumption will become scarce or disappear altogether, and the number of forest and bush fires will increase. There is a solid chance that hurricanes will become more frequent and more powerful; the monsoon cycle will be disrupted and, in general, the world's weather will become increasingly dramatic.

The retreat of glaciers will continue. There will be less snow cover on the planet, permafrost will continue to melt, the extent of sea-ice will decrease further, and the Greenland ice sheet will certainly shrink. What's more, the pace of all of these changes will increase as the pace of temperature change increases. Places which have slowly lost ice or snow cover will lose it more quickly, possibly even lose it altogether. Glacier National Park in Montana was once entirely covered with ice and snow. In 1850 there were as many as 150 glaciers in it. Now there are 27, and by 2030 the last of those will have gone. The snows of Kilimanjaro – 'unbelievably white in the sun', according to Hemingway – will vanish by 2020. At least one sixth of the world's population receives fresh water in the form of meltwater from mountain ranges. Water supplies for a large number of human beings, maybe billions, will dwindle and vanish in the decades to come.

These general changes to the weather and the planet's surface will certainly be accompanied by changes in the lives of many plants and animals. Creatures already under threat of extinction will probably be pushed over the edge by changes to the environment. It is not just the poster boys for climate change – well-known creatures like polar bears and gorillas – which are doomed. According to some estimates, anything from 15 to 37 per cent of all species of plants and animals could be locked into extinction as a result of the effects of climate change as early as 2050.[18] The rate of extinction in this century is thought to be 100 to 1,000 times greater than the usual background rate. Against the backdrop of the fossil record, we are living in the sixth major extinction event our planet has experienced – the fifth one did in the dinosaurs. The biologist E. O. Wilson has called our immediate future 'The Age of Loneliness', a time when it's us on the planet and not much else.[19] However you try to come to grips with it, we are living through a time of astonishing, sudden and permanent loss.

All of these changes will affect human beings as well, and not just human beings who, like mountain gorillas, make their homes in precarious locales. The most obvious change is just the increase in average temperatures. Some places, of course, will become more habitable, but the places which already are habitable, places we inhabit rather densely, will become less so. Deserts could march across the American Northwest. The Mediterranean might inherit the climate of North Africa.[20] Heat alone can kill us. During a heat wave in the summer of 2003, as many as 35,000 people died across Europe – some estimates put the number much higher. Whether or not the high temperatures were caused by global warming is beside the point. The fact is that warmer, sustained temperatures can kill a lot of people. The World Meteorological Association estimates that the number of people killed each year by the heat will double by 2020 as average temperatures increase.[21]

Now consider anticipated changes in sea level. Sea level will continue to rise by between 10 centimetres to a metre by the end of the century. Like globally averaged surface temperatures, the rise could be much greater in some places than others. Because the average temperature of the oceans takes much longer to change compared to surface temperatures, the thermal expansion of the oceans will take a bit of time. This means that the sea level will continue to rise for many centuries, perhaps thousands of years, no matter what we do. Almost half of the people alive today live in coastal zones, in areas which might be subject to flooding with even a small increase in global sea levels. Bangladesh, for example, is more or less a densely populated river delta. With a rise of a metre, the country would lose 20 per cent of its habitable land, land currently occupied by approximately 15 million people. Sea level in the region of Bangladesh is expected to rise by about a metre by 2050. Some estimates put the rise at 2 metres by 2100.[22]

You can wonder where all of these people are going to go – not just the people of Bangladesh but the hundreds of millions more who will be affected by sea level rises all over the world. You might also wonder what everyone is going to eat. Because the soils of flood planes are rich in nutrients, quite a bit of the planet's agricultural production happens on them, on just the places which will be lost with a rise in sea level. Industry tends to locate itself near coasts and rivers too, and it will suffer accordingly. Drinking water is in danger as well, because when sea level rises, sea water finds its way into the water table. Increasing temperatures will also have an effect on what can be grown and where it can be grown – crops will be lost while we try to adapt.

We can expect a future with hundreds of millions, even billions of displaced, hungry, thirsty people in it, escaping not just sea-level rises but on the move away from scorched croplands and empty wells. It doesn't take much to imagine conflicts happening over our planet's diminishing or shifting resources. It also doesn't take much to see that the world's poorest will be the ones most adversely affected, as well as the ones with the least resources for adaptation. Africa, for example – already a continent in the grip of drought, crop-failures, regional conflict, water shortages, disease and on and on – can expect to be made much worse off by climate change.[23]

There is going to be a lot of death in the future, a lot of death which wouldn't have happened had we and those before us acted otherwise. There will also be a lot of extra suffering, disease, thirst, hunger, violence and the like, horrors which wouldn't have happened had we and those before us acted otherwise. What we do now and in the next few years is going to matter – what this generation does is going to matter a lot – but we are getting ahead of ourselves.

All of these changes are on the cards, but scientists also talk about 'large-scale, high-impact, non-linear' changes resulting from increasing temperatures, and by this they mean planetary catastrophes. The mechanisms underpinning these changes are poorly understood, and there is no consensus as to when and in some cases if these events might occur. There is, though, at least a widespread worry that they might occur in the next century or beyond if we carry on burning fossil fuels at current levels, if we are foolish enough to carry on with business as usual.

The ocean thermohaline circulation, which some call 'the ocean conveyor', carries heat between the oceans of the world. It's responsible for the fact that northwestern Europe enjoys a milder climate for its latitude than, say, Greenland. Warm waters from the south are driven north. Part of what drives the circulation is the fact that dense, cold, salty water sinks. According to one scenario, as the world warms up, there will be more precipitation, and therefore more fresh water in the oceans, and over time this will weaken the flow of ocean currents, perhaps shutting the circulation down completely and irreversibly. The melting of the planet's ice is also releasing fresh water into the system. The distribution of heat on our planet would change dramatically, and the disruption would alter all sorts of habitats and human lives.

After decades and decades of continued warming, some time in the twenty-first century, the Antarctic ice sheet could begin to melt. If the melt is substantial, there is enough ice there to contribute to several metres of sea-level rise. The ice covering parts of Greenland is already melting, but again with sustained increases in temperature, it will melt entirely, adding as much as 7 metres to the sea level. It's a huge increase, affecting almost all parts of the planet in some way or another.[24]

Abrupt breakdowns in ecosystems could also result from continued warming. This is something over and above a large number of extinction events to which we are already committed. Instead, entire ecosystems could crash – the entire, vast Amazon rainforest might be on its way to desertification, to take just one terrible possibility – wiping out more or less every kind of creature which lives there and altering permanently the connections between that ecosystem, the climate, and the rest of the planet.

There are also a number of possible feedback mechanisms, such as water vapour feedback mentioned a moment ago. Scientists talk about thresholds, points of no return, tipping points, and after certain lines are crossed particular feedbacks kick in which drive the pace of climate change on. The increased pace itself has knock-on effects and results in still more feedbacks, and in time the climate system just gets warmer and warmer, perhaps eventually reaching a new stable state which is nothing like the temperate one we currently inhabit. The suggestion is that we have no real understanding of the location of these thresholds, but we know that we are heading in their direction. It's an echo of the thought first voiced by Revelle and Suess: we are conducting an experiment on our planet, and we have no clear idea of what the results are going to be.

James Lovelock is famous for the so-called Gaia hypothesis or view that the Earth is a self-regulating system, with parts, including living parts, which together make the planet hospitable and habitable. Lovelock has recently argued that it might well be too late to do anything substantial about climate change. Perhaps we have already crossed various lines, he worries, and the only thing we can do now is prepare for the coming horrors of a dangerously inhospitable climate. Governments should devote resources to saving as many of their people as possible. Human knowledge should be recorded in durable books which survivors might stumble upon in the wreckage of civilization. Maybe bunkers need to be built. Perhaps the most we can hope for is to help the survivors, maybe even cling to the meagre hope that our species will be among those few which manage to survive. He ends a recent book with this disturbing image:

> Meanwhile in the hot arid world survivors gather for the journey to the new Arctic centres of civilization; I see them in the desert as the dawn breaks and the sun throws its piercing gaze across the horizon at the camp. The cool fresh night air lingers for a while and then, like smoke, dissipates as the heat takes charge. Their camel wakes, blinks and slowly rises on her haunches. The few remaining members of the tribe mount. She belches, and sets off on the long unbearably hot journey to the next oasis.[25]

This part of Lovelock's thinking – there is more to his account of climate and humanity than this – constitutes a minority opinion.

While some scientists do countenance the possibility of the unavoidable near-extinction of our species as a result of climate change, the vast majority claim that reducing greenhouse-gas emissions will lessen and slow the effects of climate change.

The variation in estimates in sea level rises, average temperatures and so on have most to do with projections in the amount of carbon dioxide in the atmosphere. The various emissions scenarios used by the IPCC to predict future temperatures are characterized by the choices we make now. Some scenarios feature rapid economic growth, the introduction of efficient technologies, increasing social interaction and different sorts of energy production; others depict heterogeneous worlds with growing populations and not much in the way of co-operation, with regional winners and losers; still others place an emphasis on global solutions to sustainability; others focus on local attempts to protect both people and the environment. The storylines result in different worlds.

All of this might reassure you just a little. The one variable which seems to have the most to do with the extent of climate change is the one we can have the most immediate effect on. It's not sunspots or carbon-uptake capacity or the rate of glacial melting. It's us.

2 Right and Wrong

All the gold which is under or upon the earth is not enough to give in exchange for virtue.

Plato

The scientific facts are a necessary part of reflection on climate change, but they are nothing near the whole of it. Science can tell us what is going on, but not what we should do about it. What we should do depends largely on what we value and how we think about our values. Before we find our way into the particular moral questions associated with climate change, it makes sense to spend a little time thinking about morality as such. Obviously, there's only space enough to focus on the parts of moral philosophy which might serve as background to the arguments which are to come. In addition to providing this background, I also hope to put some misconceptions about ethics to one side – certain misconceptions about how, why and whether we can justify our moral beliefs – just as we did with some distracting thoughts about the science of climate change.

It is certainly worth saying at the start that moral philosophy depends on giving reasons for certain sorts of beliefs, offering reasoned justifications. Unless you think this kind of thing is not only possible, but that it matters a lot, the arguments in the following chapters won't move you. So we'll spend a little time with the bare possibility of justification, with why justifications matter, and the way such justifications can go. Part of the point of all of this is to emphasize the fact that being human involves living in accordance with principle. This fact will matter once we have some arguments for action on climate change before us.

It will also help to know something about a few moral theories, as well as consistency and the roles of emotion and intuition in moral reflection. Finally, a few words about environmental ethics are needed, just so you know something of the approach favoured in the rest of this book. This approach might not sit well with some conceptions of environmentalism, but the hope is that there is room for it. The problems associated with climate change are so serious that we should take whatever theoretical help we can get, but also use whatever we've got. We'll start with philosophy and the place of moral reflection in it.

PHILOSOPHY AND MORALITY

Philosophy generally conceived, whatever else it is, is a particular sort of attempt to answer three very large questions. What exists? How do we know? What are we going to do about it? Answers to the first question involve us in metaphysics, an examination of the bare bones of being. Metaphysicians try to put a little flesh on the bones by saying something about the basic categories or fundamental features of reality – the nature of God, numbers, mind, properties, causation and so on. Answers to the second question concern epistemology, the study of knowledge itself. Epistemology has as part of its subject matter the attempt to say what the conditions for knowing a proposition are, as well as when or whether we satisfy those conditions. Answers to the third question involve us in moral philosophy, in large measure, an attempt to articulate and describe the principles of ethical behaviour or right conduct.

It might be something of a relief to know that we'll be concerned with morality as opposed to the bare bones of being or the conditions of knowledge. Maybe it's a little bit of a relief to me, too.

For some of us, reflection on ethics can feel comfortable or anyway more comfortable than thinking about the ontological status of numbers or the necessary and sufficient conditions for the justification of belief. Certainly those who come to philosophy for the first time know something about ethical behaviour, even if they have never worried much about philosophy's other subject matter. We have, all of us, been brought up within a framework of beliefs which we think are simply true, maybe even beyond question or at least uncontroversial. Some of those beliefs are moral in nature. So just in virtue of our membership of some sort of family and culture, we have a share of moral beliefs. Presumably, that's where the feeling of relief comes from, but it can wear off fairly quickly.

Moral philosophy is more than just having views about right and wrong. Anyone, after all, can think that stealing is wrong, but the thought might turn into moral philosophy if it is backed up by reasons which hang together in a certain way, reasons which support it as a conclusion. The claim made a moment ago about philosophy being an attempt to answer three very large questions needs at least one amendment: the answers have to be informed by a general sort of logic or reasoning. Just saying or thinking that stealing is wrong is not doing moral philosophy – you've got to have supporting reasons for the claim. So although we all have a share of moral beliefs just because we are people brought up in a certain way, moral philosophy might really be as unfamiliar as metaphysics, because moral philosophy is not just the beliefs, but the reasons for them.

THE IMPORTANCE OF GIVING REASONS

Before we can get underway, though, it might be best to have a look at some variations on the claim that moral theory, giving reasons for our moral beliefs, just isn't possible. If you understand why giving reasons is not only possible but necessary, you'll have a better grip on moral philosophy and the role of morality in our decision making. We can then have a think about how giving reasons for moral beliefs actually works.

You might suspect that something has gone wrong in even the bare conception of moral philosophy just glanced at a moment ago. Maybe you sense a kind of tension in it. On the one hand, it seems true that we all have a set of background moral beliefs on which to draw in our thinking about right and wrong – we have this just given the way that we have been brought up. On the other, moral philosophy is thought to be in the business of giving reasons for those beliefs. It might occur to you to think that the reason we have moral beliefs has already been given: we have them because of the way we were brought up. End of story.

Thinking in this way trades on an ambiguity in the meaning of the word 'reason'. The reason, in the sense of the explanation for our having the moral beliefs that we do, really might just boil down to facts about our upbringing. However, the reason, in the sense of the rational justification of our moral beliefs, is something else entirely. If I ask you for the reason, the rational justification, for your belief that self-defence excuses some sorts of violence, and you go on about your cultural heritage, I've got room to think you missed the point of my question. What I'm after is an argument, a set of premises and a conclusion, a bit of moral philosophy in other words, not biography or history.

It's this ambiguity which makes a little sense of the rejoinder, usually accompanied by a slap to the speaker's forehead, which might be paraphrased as, 'You don't believe that just because your parents believe it, do you?' Part of the thought encapsulated here is that rational justifications for belief are something more than a story about their origins. Maybe we all inherit a set of moral beliefs, but then it's up to us to work out justifications for them – and we might well reject or modify them in the process. Some go so far as to say that failing to find our own justifications is a kind of moral failure. However you come down on the point, you need not simultaneously downplay the importance of our traditions. Some parts of a tradition might be brimming with well-articulated and well-supported conceptions of justice, fairness, equality and the like. It's as wrong to ignore all of that as it is to take it for granted. But arguing and reflecting within a tradition is not the same as blindly following it.

At any rate, you might think that the sort of justification required by moral philosophy is impossible, given a deeper notion of the origin or nature of moral beliefs, something to do with social psychology, anthropology or evolution. This is a different and slightly more sturdy thought. It might be, a version of this line of thinking goes, that morality is nothing more than a cultural arte-fact. No rational justification can be given for our moral beliefs, because there aren't any justifications of the sort to be had. Morality is nothing more than a set of rules born in our tribe's social needs and wants, rules which are what they are because they help us all get along. It might have been otherwise, in fact it is otherwise, with groups of people in other parts of the world who have different needs and agendas, different circumstances and histories.

Perhaps you are tempted by a similar but darker thought – expressed as far back as Plato and again, forcefully, in Nietzsche's writings – that morality is nothing more than the codification of the will of the strong. Some recent thinkers under the suasion of possibly dubious evolutionary reflection add a little pop Darwinism and claim that morality is the human manifestation of the rules governing monkey hierarchies. Alpha males demand certain sorts of behaviour from their simian underlings, and we've carried on with this in our own human way. Our moral codes main-tain the rulers in their position of dominance: repay your debts, don't lie or cheat, if slapped around then turn the other cheek, honour your elders and so on. Some point to uncharitable facts about our genes and draw selfish conclusions.

Either way, you might conclude that the justifications which allegedly make up a large part of moral philosophy are impossible. The lines of thinking just scouted are meant to show that, given the origins of morality in something other than reason, there are no justifications, no reasons, for our moral beliefs. Reason never really gets a foothold. We have the moral beliefs we do because of forces other than our own minds – we have been socialized or perhaps evolutionarily constrained such that we have moral codes in our heads. We don't, however, behave morally because we've followed an argument through and seen that the conclusion, do what's right, is the right thing to do. So the argument can go.

It might be that the best response to this thinking is to say that maybe it's right, maybe morality is a complicated social glue, which exists to help us get along together as best we can. Maybe it showed up first of all as rules set down by those in charge or even as the inbuilt rules of primate social behaviour or, steady yourself, our genes. But even if some or all of this is true – and I've got a strong suspicion that it isn't – even if it's the right story to tell about the origin or original function of morality, there's still plenty of room for moral philosophy.

In asking for a reasoned justification for our moral beliefs, we are recognizing a human fact, that is to say, a fact about our humanity. Wherever morality came from, whatever its first function or even its present function, its dictates have a kind of force on us only when we make them our own, when we live by and sometimes for them – only, in other words, when we accept reasons for them. If we don't manage reasons for our moral beliefs, then moral beliefs really are something shallow like social glue or the mere remnants of some simian hierarchy. When we do manage reasons, we do something more, something human, which really deserves the name 'morality'.

This thought isn't easy to get a grip on, and an example might help, even if it's a slightly silly one. The point is worth it. Kurt Vonnegut's book, *The Sirens of Titan*, tells the story of Salo, an explorer from a race of extremely long-lived robots. Salo is on a mission, carrying a message to another galaxy, when a small metal strip which is necessary for his ship's functioning breaks down, stranding him on a moon in our solar system. He requests help from his fellows far away, and they respond by focusing various beams on primordial Earth, thus manipulating its entire history, starting life on the planet and governing its direction and evolution in such a way that the point and purpose of every human life has something to do with delivering a replacement part to him. Otherwise impressive human monuments, such as the Great Wall of China and Stonehenge, are just part of the manipulation: they are messages from Salo's distant comrades, in their own geometrical language, which translate roughly as, 'It won't be long now.' A human eventually, unwittingly, delivers the part. The message Salo was carrying was a single word, 'Greetings', meant for another civilization.

The story turns up in some discussions of the meaning of life. Some argue that human life can have no real meaning without some objective, outside agency – something or someone other than us which might bestow meaning on our lives. God is the usual suspect here. The claim is that an individual might have goals or objectives, but unless those goals are part of a grand scheme, they have no meaning on their own. Maybe they are too small to matter, or perhaps they are too fleeting to have meaning, given our short spans. Some have argued that if what we do is part of an objective, extra-human, possibly divine plan, then perhaps our fleeting lives really can have meaning. Maybe we're not as doomed as we thought. What matters is the outside agency. Without it, the argument goes, human life is meaningless.

The trouble with this, brought into the light by Vonnegut's book, is that a life can have a perfectly objective purpose, even a purpose secured by an outside agency, but remain spectacularly meaningless. Every human life in Vonnegut's story has a purpose secured by an external, maybe immortal, objective outside agency, but that purpose is appalling. Everybody who ever lived played a part in a plan to deliver a little bit of metal to fix a spacecraft and enable its occupant to pass on a vapid message. Everything in Earth's history has a purpose – all the little loves and losses, as well as the large-scale 'accomplishments' of the human race – but it's hard to think there's any meaning worth having in any of those human lives.

The moral of the story, for what it's worth, is that if human life is to have a meaning, we've got to accept it or otherwise buy into it. We've got to see the point, accept it as our own, otherwise there's no point at all, objective purpose or not.

Think again about the claims concerning the origin of morality made a moment ago. Each one issues in the conclusion, on the basis of some story about the origin of morality, that we cannot have proper reasons for our moral beliefs. Maybe moral beliefs are beyond justification because they are just social artefacts, just contingent on the needs of our particular social group. Or perhaps moral beliefs are beyond justification because they are just the codified will of the strong. Think again about genes if you like.

Well, if we leave our beliefs as knee-jerk reactions, socialized or evolutionarily conditioned responses to the vagaries of life, then maybe they stay stuck as social artefacts, expressions of the will of the strong or even the 'will' of our genes. They remain pale and faded, and it's as hard to find meaning or value in them as it is to find meaning or value in a human life in Vonnegut's book. Whatever the origins of our beliefs, unless we now have reasons for them, and unless those reasons are our own, we end up without morality.

What Foot calls 'morality as it lives and breathes' is what it is, in part, because of the reasons we give and accept for our beliefs about right and wrong. Much like the pointless people in Vonnegut's book, if we don't buy into reasons for our moral beliefs, it's hard to see how they could mean a thing to us. It's moral phi-losophy, justification with reasons, which might lift mere behav-iour up from instinct and stimulus-response, and make it a good deed, a human action worthy of praise. If morality is to matter to us, then we've got to find reasons for our moral beliefs, wherever they might originate. We've got to think them through or they're nothing at all.

Most importantly, once we have thought through our moral beliefs, we have to live by them and act on them. Otherwise maybe we're nothing at all too – or at least much less than we might be. There is a hope in here about ethics and our actions, in particular what we decide to do about climate change. Maybe you can already see a conclusion or two coming, but again we are getting ahead of ourselves.

Or perhaps all of this is too high-minded for you. I admit it's thin and maybe too quick, but I get the feeling that at least some of it is true anyway. I also can't think of a better way of thinking about the connection between climate change and ethics and action. I know none of this does much to convince the die-hard sceptic, who might be tempted to dig in her heels and say that the whole line of thinking just rehearsed only works 'if morality is to matter to us'. Maybe it never will or it can't. But if you are tempted by the high-minded talk, if you think morality has to make a difference somewhere, maybe you can see why there might be some merit in not just these reflections, but also the forehead-slap, followed by the exasperated claim, 'You don't believe that just because your parents believe it, do you?' Having moral beliefs and never both-ering about the reasons for them, never seeking justifications, never thinking but merely accepting, leaves you with something less than a genuine moral outlook, something closer to meaning-lessness, something not quite human.

Failing to act in accordance with moral reasons when you have them is something probably worse than meaninglessness. Maybe it's viciousness or recklessness. Unfortunately, we'll come back to this kind of thing in Chapter 4.

JUSTIFYING MORAL BELIEFS

How might moral beliefs be justified? How does it actually work? It is sometimes claimed that everyone is entitled to their views, particularly views about right and wrong. No doubt that is true, as far as it goes, but it doesn't go all that far. What do you do with someone who thinks that killing innocent people is morally acceptable? You would have some trouble persuading me that such a person is entitled to his views. There's a difference between toleration and just letting anything fly.

Maybe you share this view of mine about innocent people and killing, and you might take a moment to wonder what justifies it. Certainly reasons can be given in its favour. It might be said that innocent people are just that, innocent, and they don't deserve harm, much less death. Maybe this thought partly rests on a hidden view, a concealed claim that some people have it coming, but leave that for a moment. What is it about innocence which leads to the conclusion that innocent people do not deserve harm?

Well, you might think that it has something to do with justice, that harming the innocent is unjust. You might stop right there – that might be enough for you – or you can press the matter further. You can lean on that thought about justice, and wonder what justice is. If you lean on it hard enough, you might come up with a very large conception of justice: unless some morally relevant considerations intervene, justice means that burdens and benefits should be distributed among people equally. All things being equal, there's nothing morally relevant about an innocent person which marks her up for extra burdens, much less the harm of killing. So killing an innocent person is quite clearly wrong, given those thoughts on justice.

Probably you can already tell what I am up to here. The above rehearsal is just an example of the justification of moral beliefs, and it is something we do fairly naturally. No doubt you already know quite a bit about this kind of justification, but it's worth making this knowledge a bit more explicit.

We chain reasons backwards, usually, when we try to think through and justify a moral belief of our own. On occasion, we seem to hit bedrock, something we accept as simply so. Maybe for you it's the claim that harming the innocent is unjust. Or perhaps you wanted more and needed an account of justice to shore up the other claims. You can pick the whole thing apart a little if you like. The original claim 'killing innocent people is wrong' was partly unpacked. What is innocence? In what sense does it matter when it comes to killing? The thought which showed up fairly quickly was one about justice, and if that thought wasn't enough, it was easy to find some further thoughts about justice and innocence. From there, the connections between thoughts about right, wrong, innocence and killing seemed as straightforward as you like.

All of this is plain enough, maybe so plain that it's unnecessary to draw it to your attention, but the obvious nature of these sorts of thought is the point. We justify moral beliefs with reasons like this all of the time. What isn't so obvious, though, is the nature of that bedrock mentioned above.

Our worries seemed to end when we secured our thinking in talk of justice. There are interesting questions here, and you can wonder about the bedrock, beliefs some people think of as ultimate or foundational, mental spaces where questioning just seems to stop. In what looks like the middle of a moral debate, sometimes both disputants just stop when agreement is suddenly reached – maybe they agree on something which seems foundational to both of them. On other occasions, the argument continues, and speculation carries on for as long as the two parties can stand it. For anything which might be the foundation of a moral belief, it can be asked, 'Well, what justifies that?' Whatever answer is given, it can be asked, again, 'Well, what justifies that?'

If, like me, you are of a certain frame of mind, you might have doubts about so-called foundations. For my part, I think you could lean on talk of justice too, if you thought it needed shoring up, and you might find more beliefs underneath it. I get the feeling that you can go as far down as you like with moral justification, as deep as you feel you need to go until you no longer find the question of justification pressing. Some draw the conclusion, from these kinds of thoughts, that moral philosophy has no foundation, and therefore our moral beliefs are somehow unsupported. Others see richness in our moral thinking, a kind of depth. You can hold your breath and go as far down into justification as you like, and you will always stand a chance of finding more supporting reasons down there. Eventually, though, you'll have to come up for air and act in the world. You would have to do that whether you hit bedrock or not.

Moral philosophy, then, involves these sorts of justifications, foundational ones or not, and a bit more. The bit more becomes clearer when you think of something other than justifying your own beliefs. Think about a moral disagreement.

A fair share of remonstration in moral matters consists in pointing out inconsistencies in an opponent's thinking. Morality, whatever else it is, insists on a kind of humane consistency. Suppose two people are arguing about the death penalty and abortion. One is in favour of the death penalty and pro-life, and the other is against the death penalty and pro-choice. You can hear it starting: 'How can you be pro-choice but against the death penalty? Why is it fine to kill babies but wrong to kill murderers?' The point is a fair one, precisely because there's a large apparent inconsistency in holding on to the claim that killing babies is acceptable and the claim that killing murderers is wrong. If both are kinds of killing, and if one kind of killing is wrong, doesn't consistency demand that the other kind is wrong too?

You can hear the reply already, and maybe it has to do with relieving the inconsistency by talk of what constitutes a person – possibly the line is that a foetus, in the early stages at least, is not a person – but a murderer is. Killing is wrong, it might be claimed, and while the death penalty is a kind of killing, abortion is not. There's no one there to be killed – no person, just some cells.

Maybe the argument goes further. The person who is pro-choice and against the death penalty might offer a counter-argument rooted in another inconsistency. 'What sense does it make to think that murder, taking a life, is so horrible that taking a life is the only response to it? Where's the consistency in that?' These lines point out another apparent and large inconsistency in a possible justification of the death penalty: killers should be killed, because taking a life is wrong. Still, if taking a life is wrong, and the death penalty is taking a life, then the death penalty is wrong too, isn't it?

Again you might be able to hear another reply, and maybe it has to do with relieving the inconsistency with talk of desert. Some killing is permissible if it's deserved. A killer's victims did not deserve their deaths, but a killer surely deserves hers. Perhaps the talk is bolstered with further claims about justice and punishment.

You have heard, maybe been involved in, debates like these. Notice that the lines pursued above involve largely moral disagreements and not factual ones. The disputes are about principles and their application, as opposed to matters of fact. Sometimes there is overlap, and what looks like a moral disagreement can be settled by pointing to facts. If I'm about to press a button which demolishes a block of flats, and someone rushes up to stop me, calling me a monster for destroying homes and killing people, maybe I can point out that he's got his facts wrong. Maybe no one lives in the buildings anymore. Given the facts, there's no moral issue here at all.

Sometimes, though, pointing to facts is the wrong thing to do, because the disagreement really is a moral one. Suppose that I say we should go to war – a nearby country has annexed a neighbour unjustly, and we should come to our neighbour's aid. You can disagree, but if the reason you give against me is a factual one, say that such a war would be expensive, I might be entitled to remain unmoved. Sometimes morality trumps the facts, and sometimes the facts are just irrelevant.

From these examples, you can probably already see the importance of consistency in our thinking about right and wrong. Consistency generally conceived is not peculiar to moral philosophy; it's fundamental to the practice of philosophy itself. You can think of it as logical consistency or the deliberate attempt to avoid contradictions. Certainly it has to do with avoiding contradictions in the reasons we give, the justifications. Moral philosophy, like any philosophy, depends on consistency in this sense, but it requires something more specific, namely, consistency of principle. If I think

I have certain duties or obligations to someone in a certain set of circumstances, then, all things being equal, consistency requires that I have just the same duties or obligations to other people in similar circumstances. If I think that I deserve treatment of a certain sort, then others in my situation deserve treatment of that sort too.

Morality is shot through with demands for this kind of consistency, and maybe it's just built into moral thinking itself. It's why 'All men are created equal' rings true, but 'All animals are equal, but some are more equal than others' does not. A quick wave at two of the most dominant moral theories in the recent history of philosophy might help make the point and, in a backhanded way, give you more of a grip on the nature of moral philosophy itself. We'll come back to both of them in due course.

CONSISTENCY, MORAL THEORIES, INTUITIONS

Utilitarianism is the view that the moral rightness or wrongness of an act depends on nothing other than the consequences of the act, and on most traditional readings those consequences are cashed out in terms of human happiness. Possibly the first serious defender of the view is Bentham. He is certainly remembered as among the first of philosophers who put rationality at the heart of morality and legislation, as opposed to simple prejudice or an appeal to the divine. He did this with a single principle: the principle of utility or the greatest happiness principle.

He says clearly what he means by it: the greatest happiness principle 'approves or disapproves of every action whatsoever, according to the tendency which it appears to have to augment or diminish the happiness of the party whose interest is in question'.[1] The principle, and the conception of happiness on which it depends, is based on a particular fact about human nature. Human beings, Bentham argues, are governed by two masters: pleasure and pain. Increasing an individual's happiness is nothing less than increasing the balance of pleasure over pain in his life. Increasing human happiness in a society, therefore, is a matter of increasing the general balance of pleasure over pain for everyone. Morality falls out of all of this quickly. Any action which conforms to the principle of utility, which augments the overall balance of pleasure over pain, ought to be done: it is morally right.

The thing to notice about this, for our purposes, is Bentham's insistence on consistency: everybody's pain and pleasure matters equally. If you want to work out whether your action is right or wrong, it's no good worrying about just your pleasure or just the pleasure to be had by your friends and family. Conversely, it's no good ignoring the pain of people who otherwise don't matter much to you. If pleasure and pain count at all, everyone's pleasure and pain count equally.

A second moral theory, which rightly gets at least as much press as utilitarianism, is Kant's conception of right and wrong. For Kant, doing the right thing is not a matter of the consequences of action, partly because there is a good chance that consequences are beyond an actor's control. Kant thought that morality is a matter of duty as opposed to something instrumental, so consequences shouldn't figure into our reflections directly. You do what is right because it is right, not because you get something in return for the action. So morality, Kant argues, cannot be hypothetical in nature, cannot be of the form, 'If you want such and such, do so and so'. Instead, its dictates must be categorical, of the form, 'Do this' or 'Don't do that'. Kant offers the following formulation of the so-called 'categorical imperative', the basis of Kantian morality: 'Act only on that maxim whereby you can at the same time will that it should become a universal law.'

An example, Kant's own, might make all of this clearer. Suppose the rent is due, and you have run out of money. You approach a friend for a loan, and he agrees, so long as you promise to repay by next week. You know there is no chance of your having enough cash to repay the loan in time, maybe you'll never be able to repay it, but you think about making the false promise anyway.

Kant argues that actions are undertaken under maxims or rules, and the rule you are contemplating is this: 'When I think I need some money, I will borrow it and promise to repay it, though I know I never can do so.' The interesting thing for our purposes is that Kant's test for such maxims is universalizability. If you want to know whether what you are contemplating is right or wrong, imagine that your maxim were to become something like a universal law of nature, automatically adopted by everybody. Would the system thus engendered be consistent or self-contradictory?

If the world which results is consistent, you are in no danger of doing the wrong thing, but if that world somehow breaks down, you are in violation of the moral law. Think of it this way: if everybody made false promises, promising itself would be impossible. Who would believe a promise? The maxim you were contemplating results in a self-contradiction – the very act of making a promise would undermine itself – and it is therefore not in keeping with the categorical imperative. So you shouldn't do it. For Kant, everything turns on the possibility of the consistent application of moral principles.

Before you end up with the conclusion that moral philosophy is nothing more than the consistent application of some lofty principle or other, it's worth noting that there are other conceptions of morality. It's not all just Bentham and Kant. It might help, too, to reflect a little on the role of both emotion and intuition in moral thinking. Both have long histories behind them.

Whatever else is going on when we try to work out the justifications for our moral beliefs, have a moral disagreement, or engage in full-blown moral theorizing, emotions play some sort of role. Hume argues that sympathy, our capacity to somehow share in the happiness and misery of others, moves each one of us. While reason can give us a grip on the facts of the matter, say, the consequences of our actions, it is ultimately sentiment which leads us to conclusions about right and wrong. Reason might guide our actions, but only feelings can nudge us to act in some way rather than another. Ultimately, only emotion can lead us to judge that a person is right or wrong or to take some action because it is right. We'll come back to Hume when we worry about a certain feature of problems associated with climate change, but for now we can stop just with the thought that emotions can and do feature in moral reflection.

Intuitions are no less important, but much harder to pin down. Some philosophers try for something a little too snazzy in this connection, something too good to be true, namely a faculty in us which we can use to intuit or just 'see' moral truths. Moral intuition, it is argued, can tell us whether an action is right or wrong in much the same way as vision can tell us whether a pair of suede shoes are blue. But you do not need to buy into this mess to talk sensibly about moral intuitions. You can think of them as responses or reactions to the facts, anyway something less grand than a faculty. Moral intuitions, in this sense, are almost indispensable features of thinking through moral philosophy.

Philosophers make use of thought experiments, and moral philosophers are no exception. You can think of a thought experiment as a kind of philosophical test tube. Just as an actual test tube enables a chemist to keep the rest of the world separate from what interests her, a thought experiment can force us to focus our attention on a particular concept or principle or the like. With a real test tube, you can experiment on what you are interested in and nothing else. With a thought experiment, you can tease away distractions and force yourself to consider just what might matter most. The intuitions or responses you have to thought experiments can tell you about how your concepts fit together, how you really think about something or other. A thought experiment can force consistency on you. We'll consider a few in this book.

ENVIRONMENTAL ETHICS

There is one last consistency worth thinking about now, a consistency which forms the basis of at least some versions of environmental ethics. A large part of ethical theory, as we have seen, depends on a concern for others. If it occurs to you to wonder why other people should matter so much, lots of answers are readily available. Try just these: causing pain is wrong; treating people as a means to an end is wrong; ignoring the interests of others is wrong. All such thoughts turn up with regularity in moral reflection. For just about any answer you like, however, consistency might demand that you apply your ethics to animals too.

Lots of creatures can feel pain, and if it's wrong to cause pain, it must be wrong to cause them pain as well. If it is wrong for me to treat my fellows just as a means to my goals – if I ought not to use other people to get what I want – it must be wrong to treat my fellow creatures simply as a means too, say as a means to a new fur coat. If we rightly say that other people's interests, goals and wants should figure into our moral thinking, and if animals have interests, then we should also think about those interests too. Animals might not be able to put their interests into words, but the creatures out there are all up to something – they hunt and hide and mate and build nests and have young and so on. They have interests in some sort of sense, a sense not too distant from the one I mean when I say that I have interests. Why should my interests count and not theirs?

The upshot is, roughly, that finding a moral difference between what are just different animals, us and them, is not easy. Some might argue that it is just not possible. If you have some difference in mind – something about the importance of your humanity or your rational potential or your capacity to appreciate some things and not others – be careful that you are not begging the question, presupposing just what is at issue. It's possible that the difference you have settled on is really an expression of species prejudice, a bit of human chauvinism, or so it can seem. Why should your rational capacities make a moral difference, count for more than the properties peculiar to any other animal you might care to mention?

Not all theorizing in environmental ethics makes use of the thoughts above, in fact this way of putting things is probably nearly outdated, but it does serve to get us thinking along lines of environmental values. Drawing those lines makes up the bulk of environmental ethics, because environmental ethics is largely in the business of expanding our conception of value or at least the number of things that we value. Some environmentalists make the point by emphasizing the fact that the moral sphere has been expanding for a while. People who do not own land, slaves, women, foreigners, the mentally ill, the physically handicapped and others have all been outside of the moral circle, and as we better understand the nature of right and wrong, we redraw that circle and let more and more people in. The line of thinking above might lead you to the conclusion that animals should be included too, should be brought into the moral community.

However, many thinkers in this neck of the woods object to the consistency arguments run above and argue that the mere similarity to human beings cannot be the basis for a full-blooded environmental ethic. The connections can get us going, but we really end up somewhere else entirely. What's needed is a new conception of value, something which departs from the old human framework, maybe leaves it far behind. The old framework has as part of its structure the view that human beings are the measure of things – we somehow bring value into the world.

This sort of value is of two kinds: intrinsic and instrumental, and both have everything to do with us. Some things in the world are of instrumental value, which is to say that they are good as our means, good instruments. They serve us well in our efforts to secure something else which we are really after. Other things have intrinsic value, a value we find in the objects or things themselves. On this view, human beings bring value into the world, either by valuing some things as means to our ends or by judging that other things are valuable just in themselves. A ham sandwich might be instrumentally valuable in securing something else of value, namely the pleasure of a full stomach. A Bach concerto might be of value just in itself. Certainly a human life has intrinsic value.

Why?

Probably you noticed that you were just handed a loaded example: a ham sandwich is made out of an animal. Animals in particular, and nature in general, end up as almost entirely instrumentally valuable according to this line of thinking, and the line of thinking is an old one. You can hear it as far back as Aristotle: 'nature has made all things specifically for the sake of man'.[2] Many religions suggest that some god or other created us first and then created animals and the rest of the world for us, for our use. Some thinkers have tried to locate intrinsic value in nature, by drawing attention to the beauty of a sunset or the majesty of a storm. Even if nature is credited with this sort of intrinsic value, it's still bestowed by us.

The old view is hard to shake. Even in the modern period, philosophers have stuck to it. Descartes seems to have thought that animals were soulless or at least without what we would call 'minds', incapable of feeling pleasures or pains, mostly because they couldn't speak. They were mechanisms, automata. Kant himself seems to stumble, arguing that animal cruelty is wrong not because animals are anything more than instrumentally valuable, but because roughing up your horse might give you an insensitive character and make you more likely to rough up a person.

Environmental ethics only really got going as recently as the 1960s and 1970s, and although it has always been concerned with interactions between human beings and the environment, for some its principle aim has been to get past the limits of anthropocentric valuations, to shake free of the old views. Attempts to accomplish this aim have been of two types. First, philosophers have tried to extend human values – say utilitarian or Kantian thinking, or the dictates of virtue ethics – to other creatures.[3] For example, one might come around to the view that animals have an inner life and conclude that their pains ought to figure into our efforts to maximize pleasure and minimize pains. Second and more radically, there has been a call for new values or for the valuation of new things, things in addition to or other than us.

Some argue for biocentrism, the view that every living thing has a good of its own, and that the attainment of such goods is of intrinsic value.[4] The individualism of this sort of thinking, some hasten to point out, is another holdover from an outmoded, humanistic ethic. Instead, whole species, maybe the biosphere as such, even the planet as a whole ought to be thought of as the locus of value.[5] Note that this is something more than or at least different from the claim that such things should matter to us instrumentally. It might even be something more than the claim that such things should matter to us in other familiar ways. The hope might be to get us out of the equation, in a certain sense, maybe to move to a more objective, non-human kind of valuation.

For some, these final, radical thoughts are just too much. It is difficult to swallow, even for those with sympathy for the general claims of many conceptions of environmentalism. The difficulty can become a little clearer if you think about the sorts of questions we are asking when we ask about the connection between environmental concerns and human values. As Williams points out, it is one thing to ask whose questions these are, and another to ask whose values should figure into the answers.[6] The questions, of course, are human questions, our questions. The answers are going to have to be human too. No one but us is in a position to answer them. At bottom, the answers have to make some sense to us, and this means at the very least that they have to be somehow connected to human values, values which are part of our lives, part of how we understand ourselves, part of what guides our best actions. This is not to say that the answers will represent only human interests. In making this good promise, though, you run into a difficult question: how can we value something outside of our interests?

Obviously, I can value something other than my own interests – sometimes morality requires it, demands it. But the question is whether or not I can value something other than or outside of human interests as such. Can the boat be pushed out that far? Would it even be a boat any more? There is a human perspective, and it's a familiar point that we cannot crawl outside of it. Perhaps there are some calls for a new ethic which we simply cannot heed. Or maybe we can only aim to heed them someday, perhaps work our way towards them and hope for wisdom. Radical environmentalism can strike a chord even in the mind of the most dubious. It can kindle a hope. The conclusion of human morality can't just be that only humans matter.

Working out why this strikes a chord, finding a way to act on this hope, understanding other ways of mattering, all of this is worth pursuing. There are tough questions here and good ones, but I propose to leave them for another time. Climate change raises a number of difficult moral questions, and some of them are new or can seem new. The radical thinkers among us will say that an entirely new ethic is required if we are to deal with them. Maybe new values are needed; perhaps we will find it necessary to redraw the moral circle to include much more than animals; we might have to rethink ethics and the nature of valuation. Or maybe something less is required – perhaps we'll just have to shift around the values we already have or see them in a new light.

There is, anyway, plenty of room for all of these thoughts. There is room for reflection on new values and room for what interests me most in all of this: questions about us and the values we already have. As we'll see in the next chapter, even finding our way into the challenges of climate change requires new thinking, but maybe we can stop short of needing brand new values. Some will argue that old ways of thinking got us into this mess. Nevertheless, I think we can go some way with the moral philosophy we've got.

As we have seen in this chapter, the values we have are largely built on consistency, but consistency isn't all there is to it. Principles of the sort we have glanced at – the greatest happiness principle, Kant's principle of universalizability, and lesser principles having to do with justice and innocence – are not the full story either. I have left out a lot, and some might say that I've left out what matters. We've spent our time on what's called 'normative ethics', the attempt to articulate standards or rules by which to judge the rightness or wrongness of action, even to determine the right course of action. We've almost ignored meta-ethics, the effort to work out the meaning of our normative language. Philosophy, recent philosophy anyway, has had a lot to say about meta-ethics, but it's not our principal concern here. Other large topics have been left to the side too.

We do, though, have enough to make a start. If you didn't before, by now I hope you have a grip on the part of moral philosophy which deals with justification, and I also hope you have come around to the view that those justifications are not just possible, but that they matter. Without them, a good chunk of what it is to be human just fades away. You should have a handle on how the justification of a moral claim can go. Maybe you also see why acting in accordance with morally justified belief matters too. Finally, you probably know enough about environmental ethics to know where this book fits in that story.

So we'll start where just about any practical moral enquiry has to start. We'll consider responsibility and climate change.

3 Responsibility

No snowflake in an avalanche ever feels responsible.

Voltaire

Here are some easy ones for you. Suppose I creep into an antiques shop, covet a fine vase and shoplift it. Just given that information you can come to the nearly instantaneous conclusion that what I did was wrong. Now suppose that I go into the shop, get into an argument with the shopkeeper, and smash the vase to spite him. Again, you probably think what I did was wrong. Imagine now that I'm in the same shop, but this time I'm quite drunk, and I stagger into the vase, smashing it to the ground. There's a wrong in here some-where – maybe the wrongness isn't just in the smashing of the vase, which is nearer an accident now, but closer to my letting myself get so helplessly drunk in the first place. Suppose now that I steal the vase, but you discover that I'm doing so because an art collector has kidnapped my elderly aunt, promising to dispatch her unless I deliver the vase. Clearly the collector is wrong, but maybe you are willing to let me off in this instance. Or suppose I smash the vase, but you learn that I've just received some horrible news and I'm not quite myself. Perhaps I've just discovered that the shopkeeper has been spreading vile rumours about me, rumours that have ruined my life. What if I received a knock on the head just before walking into the shop, and I now suffer from some sort of brain injury which explains my erratic behaviour? The situation is less clear in these last few examples, but you know how to start thinking about them.

In all of these cases, you know what matters and what doesn't when it comes to the moral evaluation of action. If you don't know immediately who did wrong and why, as well as what ought to be done about it, you know where to look for clarification.

Now try this one. Suppose that many millions of people use electricity to heat and cool their homes, watch television, read by bedside lights at night before falling asleep, and have hot showers and toast in the morning. They drive to work. Once a year they fly to the beach for a well-deserved weekend break, and maybe the food they eat at the beachside bar has travelled even further than they have, although they've never heard of food miles. Fossil fuels are burned in order to create the energy which drives all of these activities. This puts greenhouse gases into the atmosphere, and those gases contribute to the warming of the planet. The warming raises the sea level several thousand miles away from the televisions and the showers, many years in the future, maybe decades or even hundreds of years. The rising sea renders the drinking water in a coastal village in China unsafe. Crops wither, animals die, and lots of people who are not yet born will starve to death.

What matters and what doesn't to the moral evaluation of this sort of case? There's harm, but whose fault is it? What should be done about it? The answers are not obvious, at least not as obvious as in the examples involving that vase. What differentiates the two kinds of case?

Jamieson argues that the part of our value system which fails us in this connection has much to do with responsibility.[1] We are accustomed to thinking about individual, easily identified harms which are local, right in front of us in both space and time. It's hard for us to miss that broken vase or the fact that I broke it out of spite. I'm responsible to the tune of exactly one vase. I should be blamed and made to compensate the shopkeeper. Maybe I should pay a bit more besides, to help convince me that smashing up other shops would be a bad idea too.

All of that is plain enough, but the trouble with climate change, Jamieson argues, is that our usual paradigm collapses under the weight of certain complexities. Our values grew up in a low-tech, disconnected world of plenty. Now, cumulative and apparently innocent acts can have consequences undreamt of by our forebears. Further, the effects of actions, as well as the actions themselves, are smeared out in space and time in confusing ways. As Jamieson puts it, 'no one intended the bad outcome or brought it about or was even able to foresee it.'[2] There's no vandal standing there right in front of a broken vase. Who do we blame? Who should be made to pay? When thinking about the vase, the answers were almost instantaneous; now it's hard even to know where to begin. We can make some headway by getting the complexity itself on the table.

AGENCY AND SPATIAL AND TEMPORAL COMPLEXITIES

What's clear is that climate change involves harm. As we saw in the first chapter, as the planet warms, weather systems change. The harm won't be evenly spread: some places will become more habitable, but many more will face new extremes of weather. Sea levels will rise, flooding homes and destroying crops. Elsewhere, water shortages will threaten. Disease will spread to new areas. There will be conflict. A lot of people will die or be uprooted or suffer in other ways. Species will disappear. Whole ecosystems might well be destroyed. There are enormous harms before us. If the harms are obvious, much of the rest of the ethical dimension of climate change is obscure.

Gardiner identifies three aspects of climate change which make thinking about it particularly difficult for us.[3] There are global features of climate change: the relevant causes and effects and the agents behind them are spatially dispersed throughout the globe. There are intergenerational aspects too: the relevant causes and effects and the agents involved are temporally dispersed. Finally, reflection on the problems attending climate change is hampered by our theoretical ineptitude which, when combined with the spatial and temporal features of climate change, can lead to a kind of moral corruption. Let's start with the global aspect of climate change and work through all of this.

Considered globally, climate change is a spatial problem, with contributing causes and effects, agents and institutions, spread out over the planet. The fact that it's lots of different people, governments and businesses doing many different things in different countries compounds the trouble when we try to understand and do something about climate change. There's no one standing red-faced next to a broken vase. Actions set in motion in one hemisphere have effects on the other side of the world. The way land is used here affects flooding over there. The fuel burned over there changes the effects of the El Niño a little, which causes a drought somewhere else. Climate, it almost goes without saying, is global.

There are temporal complications too, and this issues in what Gardiner calls 'intergenerational' aspects of the problem. Causes and effects are smeared out in time as well as space. Among other things, this means that it takes a while for our actions to be translated into noticeable effects on the climate. By the time we can see some of the effects – large rises in sea level, for example – the inertia of the climate system is such that it will be too late to do something about it. Worse than this, from the point of view of coming to grips with the moral dimension of climate change, agency itself is spread out over time. There is a sense in which my actions and the actions of my present fellows join with the past actions of my parents, grandparents and great-grandparents, and the effects resulting from our actions will still be felt hundreds, even thousands of years in the future.

It is also true that we are, in a way, stuck with the present we have because of our past. The little actions I undertake which keep me warm and dry and fed are what they are partly because of choices made by people long dead. Even if I didn't want to burn fossil fuels, I'm embedded in a culture set up to do so. Short of moving off to a yurt somewhere, I can seem kind of stuck with the system when it comes to satisfying even my basic needs.

The spatial and temporal smearing of actions and agency can be deeply confusing, because sometimes moral responsibility depends conceptually on another sort of responsibility: causal responsibility. If we know that an action is wrong, then all we need to know is that someone did it in order to conclude that they were responsible for something wrong. However, the causal connections underpinning climate change are bizarre in several ways, and this muddies the waters when we try to think about who did what. It is unclear, for example, that any particular action of mine is causally responsible for any future harm. All the little things that I do today – flicking on a few light bulbs, putting my clothes in the dryer, listening to the Shipping before I go to bed – might amount to nothing more than a negligible amount of damage to the atmosphere. It is almost as though I am jointly responsible, with a million other people, for a billion little actions, in a trillion little moments. Each act is nothing in itself, each person does no obvious wrong, but together the results are catastrophic.

Given all of this, it's no wonder that a third aspect of the problem, our theoretical ineptitude, makes matters even worse. We're not much good at thinking about our long-term future, non-human animals and nature, the value of persons who might never exist, spatially and temporally smeared actions and so on. We have been able to get about our business without worrying much about any of this, so now that it matters, we lack both the wisdom and the theory to cope with it. It's possible, Gardiner concludes, that our theoretical failure can lead to a moral failure, a kind of deception in which we focus on one part of the problem and not others. The complexity can be an excuse, a problematic excuse, for doing nothing at all.

THE PRISONER'S DILEMMA AND THE TRAGEDY OF THE COMMONS

A way to make our theoretical failings as well as certain features of our thinking about both the spatial and temporal aspects of the problem a bit more concrete is to think about two famous thought experiments and apply them to the problems posed by climate change. The first is the prisoner's dilemma, and it has many incarnations. Almost all of them make plain a certain worrying feature of individual as against collective rationality.[4]

Imagine that Bonnie and Clyde are arrested for bank robbery and placed, brooding, into separate cells. They face ten years in prison if convicted, but the police, who are short on evidence, are willing to offer them a deal. They can confess, stitch up the other prisoner, and get themselves out of trouble. If one rats out the other and the other keeps quiet, the rat goes free and the other gets the full ten years. If they rat each other out, they both get five years. If they both keep quiet, though, there's nothing the police can do, and they are held only for a month on some lesser charge. They can't confer, so what should they do?

If all that matters to them is jail time, then being a rat is the right thing to do. Clyde might reason thus. 'If Bonnie keeps quiet, then the best thing to do is betray her, because then I walk. If Bonnie rats me out, then the best thing to do is still to betray her, because then at least I get only five years, not the full sentence. Either way, the right thing to do is talk.' Clyde's reflections are interesting, if not disquieting, because while co-operating is the collectively rational thing to do for both prisoners, defection and betrayal is the individually rational thing to do. If everyone co-operates, then the least time is served overall. If individuals do what's individually rational, however, they can end up undermining what's best for everyone.

Here's a second and nearby example called the 'tragedy of the commons'.[5] Suppose that instead of straightforward co-operation we are thinking about the use of some common, limited resource. Imagine five cowboys, each with ten excellent cows grazing on land held in common by all. If all that matters to the cowboys is the value of their individual herds, then each will do what he can to have as many cows as possible. Suppose that the common field is standing at full cow capacity – it can only comfortably support the 50 healthy cows happily mooing and munching away on it right now. Still, the individually rational choice for any given cowboy is to add more cows to his herd. This lowers the value of all the animals in the field – they get less to eat and become a bit scrawny – but he gets the full value of the extra cows all to himself. Everybody suffers from over-grazing – each cow is now worth less – but only the individual cowboy gets the benefits of adding more cows to his herd. The tragedy of the commons is, roughly, that it seems in everyone's indi-vidual interest to exploit a common resource as far as possible, to the detriment of the group's collective interest.

Here is one last example, a variation on the prisoner's dilemma.[6] Suppose that Bonnie and Clyde have managed to unlock the mys-teries of time travel, and they and their gang are now robbing banks throughout time. They come to the attention of the Time Cops, who manage to arrest all of them at different points in the timeline. The cops offer them the usual deal: betray the others or keep quiet, and the same system of rewards and penalties applies as before. Now that the annoying leaps through time have been put to a stop and the temporal order is re-established, the cops start grilling Robber One in 1950. They've got to wait until 1970 to brace Robber Two. Bonnie awaits interrogation in 2000; Clyde is sometime in the 2010s, and so on, up to Robber Twelve in 3005. Should the prisoners keep quiet or confess?

If the usual prisoner's dilemma indicates that it's individually rational for one prisoner to rat out another, this temporal version presents a slightly different picture. If all that matters is jail time, it is in the interest of everyone who comes earlier to rat out anyone who comes after. In fact, the ones who come earlier are not in much obvious danger from the ones who come later – they might even be dead by the time a later robber gets the chance to squeal. Again, it seems individually rational for the prisoners not to co-operate with one another, even though it would be better collec-tively (for just about everyone) to do so.

These examples can lead to a number of conclusions. Aspects of the problems attending reflection on climate change seem to fit both versions of the prisoner's dilemma and the tragedy of the commons. States thinking about obeying the terms of treaties like Kyoto are in something like the position of a prisoner reflecting on betraying a former colleague. Acting in your own interests, polluting and enjoying the benefits of untrammelled energy use, can seem like the individually rational thing to do – particularly if, so far as you know, that's what the other guy is going to do. Exploiting a common resource, like the carbon-absorbing properties of the planet, can seem like a good idea too. Everybody shares in the loss of the common resource, but only the polluter enjoys the benefits of using extra energy and dumping more carbon dioxide into the atmosphere. Even better, instead of other cowboys counting your herd and holding you responsible for the suffering of their animals, it's future generations who are really going to bear the costs. As some are still playing on swings and the rest haven't been born yet, they are unlikely to object.

At the very least, these examples show that sometimes individual and collective interests can diverge dramatically. This can only exacerbate our efforts to think our way through the problem of climate change, particularly if you bear in mind the fact that doing something about greenhouse-gas emissions will require almost unprecedented global co-operation. Intergenerational co-operation is also going to be required – earlier generations are going to have to shoulder burdens for benefits they won't be around to enjoy. Individuals, and you can think of individual states or businesses here as well if you wish, seem likely to undermine themselves and the rest of us by pursuing their own interests. Certainly those in the future, whose interests are not represented by anyone alive today, stand a good chance of being ratted out by all of us.

There is a ray of light in here somewhere. You might have noticed that, in order to get the examples going, certain turns of phrase were required. I had to set both versions of the prisoner's dilemma up with the phrase, 'if all that matters is jail time'. The tragedy of the commons would not have been so tragic without the specification that cowboys care only about the cash value of their herds. There is something funny, too, in contrasting individual and collective rationality. Talk of individual rationality seems to confine my thoughts to nothing more than what's maximally best for me, as opposed to what's best for all of us, or even just what I can put up with without too much trouble. I suppose if you put a prisoner in a room, hand her a slide-rule, confine her thoughts to what's best for her and ensure that she thinks that all that matters is jail time, then you do get something like this divergence. But isn't there a chance that what's best for everyone might figure in the reflections of a prisoner or a cowboy? Is there honour, even among thieves? Must Clyde be so selfish? Didn't he love Bonnie?

There is a large discussion or debate between some philosophers and economists about the sorts of values which should matter here, a debate which I will only mention and then quickly side-step for now.[7] Part of the disagreement has to do with whether economics is the right sort of tool, employing the right set of values, for deciding some of the meatier questions arising from the fact of climate change. There's no doubt that some questions are amenable to economic analysis, but there is considerable doubt that all questions of interest have economic answers. Philosophers jibe more than a little, insisting that moral values can and do trump talk of monetary costs, rational actors and cost-benefit analysis.

To take one obviously unfair and heinous example, which at least makes the point quickly, a few economists have tried to calculate some of the 'non-market impacts' of climate change by assigning a value to a human life in proportion to national per capita gross domestic product. You get solid and objective answers to your questions through this assignation, but you also have to think about a Chinese person as worth about one tenth of a European. We'll look away from this example, and just say that economics has to matter, but it can't matter without the careful consideration of value, which has to happen further upstream than economic analysis. Costs and benefits and rational action matter because other things matter more. Those other things are part of the ray of light we just noticed.

The ray of light can look a little feeble, however, particularly if you furrow your brow and think about actual human behaviour. Think about the bare possibility of collective, collaborative action on the part of governments and businesses which are designed for competition. Think about the objections of people who go on about practicality and solutions for the real world. Encouraging examples of intergenerational co-operation on a global scale between governments as well as industries do not spring immediately to mind. But what stands a chance of getting it going, from a certain point of view, is exactly what makes me conclude that Clyde would never squeal. Talk of rational self-interest and cost-benefit analysis gets a lot of press, but economic reasons are not the only reasons one might have. In fact, we do not act just in our own interests – thieves can be stand-up guys and cowboys can do the right thing. In the case of climate change, it can help if we think a little about what doing the right thing is and, in particular, who should be doing it.

We'll spend some time thinking about individual duties and responsibilities with respect to climate change in the last chapter. Meanwhile, our focus will be on states and their moral responsibilities. We'll start with the bare responsibility for action – if something should be done, who should do it? This question can be approached with three temporal directions in mind: the past, the present and the future. The moral demand for action on the part of some parties might arise given past behaviour, given the current distribution of resources, or given obligations to future generations. More factors could figure in our thinking, but we have more than enough to make a start.

HISTORICAL PRINCIPLES OF JUSTICE

There is a large literature on the nature of justice, and it goes as far back as Plato. You'll be as relieved as I am to know that I'm not about to rehearse it or offer up some theory of justice here. There are plenty of those.[8] Justice, however characterized, figures in talk of punishment and the distribution of goods, as well as corrective or compensatory action. Punishment might be considered just if it fits the crime, if a genuinely guilty person has to pay a fine or give up a share of freedom in proportion to the harm she caused in doing wrong. The distribution of drinking water from a common well might be thought just if it goes to everyone equally, or perhaps to those who most need it first. If we find out that extra water has been going to someone who has been taking a secret share for himself everyday, compensatory or corrective justice might demand that he give the water back or refrain from taking an equal share of water for a time in the future.

In all of these cases, conceptions of justice can seem to have something in common, and usually the common ground has to do with how goods, resources, burdens, benefits or some such are divvied up. Justice seems to consist in sharing something out equally – whether the something is a burden or a benefit – unless there are good reasons to the contrary, good grounds for departing from this default approach. The good grounds will probably have to be morally relevant grounds. Maybe you should get more water from the common well if it hasn't rained much on your crops. Without the extra share, you and those who depend on you stand a chance of suffering. Avoiding that suffering is morally relevant. So if everyone else can cope, you should get a bit more. If supplies are limited and everyone depends on the well, probably you don't get more water if you just want it for your Jacuzzi.

The morally relevant grounds for a just departure from equality can sometimes be historical or backwards-looking. As in the example above, corrective or compensatory justice demands that someone sneaking extra water in the past should give up a share of it at least until equality is re-established. Sometimes, though, a departure from equality happens for entirely different reasons. It might be agreed upon or otherwise earned. Perhaps you and your shipmates are given an equal ration of rum each night. If one agrees to take your watch in exchange for your tot of rum, the distribution of rum is no longer equal, but a glance at your history can tell us that it's just. You've departed from the default practice of an equal share for all, but you've done so for a perfectly good reason: all parties came to a mutually beneficial agreement and consented to the departure.

So historical considerations can matter a lot to the conclusions one reaches about whether the current distribution of benefits or burdens is a just one. Further, historical considerations can tug in two directions. Reflection on the history of an unequal distribution can lead to the conclusion that the distribution is just, certainly if morally relevant considerations have led up to the distribution as it now stands. Reflection on the history of an unequal distribution can also lead to the conclusion that the distribution is unjust, particularly if no relevant considerations for the inequality can be found.

If the distribution of a limited resource is not just, often a further case can quickly be made for the claim that those enjoying undeserved benefits now have a responsibility to do something about the distribution. In particular, those who have unjustly benefited might have a moral responsibility to push the distribution towards equality. Possibly corrective justice demands that some additional burdens are shouldered by those who got away with extra benefits in the past.

Think less about rum and more about greenhouse gases. We know that human beings have been pumping greenhouse gases into the atmosphere, willy-nilly, since the Industrial Revolution. If the planet could absorb everything we put up there, then it would be hard to see how the kinds of questions about justice which we have been pursuing could arise with respect to climate change. Justice of a sort only seems to matter when we are dealing with the distribution of a finite resource. If we had as much rum as we could drink, we'd have some problems to deal with, certainly, but maybe we wouldn't have to worry much about what counts as an equal distribution of rum. However, we now know that the carbon sinks of our world are finite: the planet can only absorb a certain amount of our emissions, and the rest contributes to a blanket which heats up the planet. We also know that we have already put more gases into the atmosphere than the planet can absorb without warming up.

Many philosophers now think of the carbon sinks or the absorptive properties of the planet as a finite, common resource – much like the common well in the examples above.[9] And just like that well, there is a sense in which the carbon sinks are a necessary resource, at least a resource which matters more than might be thought. Many of the people on the planet depend on fossil fuels for more than just keeping their DVD players on standby. Given the way many of our societies are set up – in particular, given our methods of energy production – putting carbon into the atmosphere is a fundamental part of securing food, shelter, warmth and other necessities. Using up someone else's share of the sink, from a certain point of view, is as unjust and as harmful as using up their water or the resources they need to build a home or produce food.

Further, it is clear that we have departed from an equal distribution of this limited resource. Not all countries emit the same amount of greenhouse gases or otherwise use an equal share of the sink. Brace yourself for some numbers. Human beings put about 26 gigatons (26 billion metric tons) of carbon dioxide into the atmosphere each year.[10] The United States is responsible for more than 20 per cent of annual global emissions; China for nearly 15 per cent, and the European Union for around 14 per cent. The next in line is Russia, with a lot less: about 5 per cent of global emissions. Even if we think in terms of per capita emissions, the distribution is not equitable at all. In 2003, for example, the US emitted almost 20 tonnes of carbon per person. Russia emitted more than 10 tonnes per capita. Countries like Vietnam, Pakistan and Chad emitted much less than one metric ton per capita. For some countries, there are no measurable greenhouse gas emissions at all.

Historically, the distribution of emissions has never been equal. Current global emissions echo cumulative emissions – the disparities are similar.[11] The US comes first on the list, responsible for almost 30 per cent of cumulative carbon-dioxide emissions between 1850 and 2002. The European Union is second, accounting for 26.5 per cent; Russia is third with 8.1 per cent; China is fourth with 7.6 per cent; within the EU, Germany comes next with 7.3 per cent; followed by the UK with 6.3 per cent. The UN's Food and Agriculture Organization categorizes countries as developed or developing. If we follow these groupings, then developed countries are responsible for over 800,000 million metric tons of carbon emitted since 1900. The developing world, including huge countries like China and India, has contributed much less: just over 213,000 million metric tons. Since 1850, the developed world is responsible for a total of 76 per cent of carbon-dioxide emissions, while the developing world has contributed just 24 per cent. Based on the World Bank's grouping of countries as high income or low income, high-income countries have produced 617,000 million metric tons of carbon dioxide, while low-income countries are responsible for just 51,000 million metric tons. The rest has been emitted by countries somewhere in between.

So are there any morally relevant historical grounds for the present unequal use of the planet's common carbon sinks? Should we be tugged in the direction of thinking that the current set-up is a morally defensible one? Certainly there have been no relevant and mutually beneficial agreements between developed and developing countries, as there were in the case of you and your shipmates. But there might be other grounds for thinking that certain inequalities are nevertheless justified.

Singer considers two arguments for the claim that an unequal distribution might nevertheless be morally acceptable.[12] The model is private property or instances in which some people take part of what might have been held in common for themselves. There is at least one tradition, owed to Locke, which comes around to the conclusion that an unequal distribution of a common resource can be better for all concerned than an equal distribution. Locke suggests that we consider the situation of the Native

American of Locke's time, whose society, he says, is set up such that there is no private property, no private ownership of land, and therefore no organized cultivation. Certainly, no one has appropriated a common resource here – there is no unjust departure from equality – but then again, Native Americans do not have much in the way of stuff, particularly foodstuffs, or so Locke maintains.

Consider now the situation in Locke's England. There, over time the common ground has been appropriated by landowners with large estates, and landless labourers work the land. The common resource, the land, has been taken up by individuals, and the distribution is not equal at all, but the day labourer has no ground for complaint. Even the best-off Native American, Locke maintains, has less food, worse lodgings and poorer shelter than the landless worker in England. The English set-up is not equal, but there is a sense in which everyone benefits.

Singer rightly notices that the factual basis of Locke's comparison is more than just rough around the edges, but even if we look away from this, the situation with the planet's carbon sinks is very different from the case of private land use. Locke seems to argue that, however it came about, the current set-up has seen to it that the average Englishman has more than the average Native American. Even if any given Native American has an equal share of the land, even an equal share of whatever is going, there's less going, precisely because there's no private ownership driving production. The unequal distribution of land in England gets trumped by something morally relevant: the workers and the owners in England all benefit from increased productivity. English lives are arguably better than they would have been had a system with equal shares prevailed.

However, Singer notes, even if everyone benefits from landowners taking more than an equal share of the land, not everyone benefits from developed countries taking more than their share of the global sinks. For a start, most of the people in poorer countries cannot hope to afford what gets produced by the rich nations' high-energy economies. Not many people in East Timor can afford a new, top-of-the-line refrigerator. This has not stopped rich nations charging poorer ones for things like medicine and agricultural equipment, which is partly the reason why poor countries have racked up enormous debts. As Shue rightly points out, the poor have mostly paid for whatever benefits have trickled down to them.[13] Further, developing countries are harmed and will be harmed in all sorts of ways as a result of the developed countries emitting greenhouse gases. It might be true that an English labourer had more meat on the table in Locke's day than a Native American. In our day and in future days, there will be less meat, even less tables, for many people in the developing world as a result of the unequal emission of greenhouse gases.

The second argument Singer considers is owed to Adam Smith. Smith argues that the rich have something of a right to their wealth, because their wealth does not deprive the poor of much and brings to the poor certain benefits. The rich, on this account, 'take only what is most precious' and divide with the poor the fruits of 'all their improvements'. Smith's well-known invisible hand ensures that necessities are distributed more or less as they would have been had things just been divided equally. The rich do not consume all that much more than the poor consume, and, anyway, they take only the most precious things, items which wouldn't really be missed by the average poor person anyway. Further, in pursuit of their wealth, the rich set up a world with many more goods in it. Like Locke, Smith thinks that just splitting things up equally leaves the average person with less than she would have if the rich get to keep some things for themselves.

Again, the analogy breaks down almost immediately. If we think about carbon sinks, it is just not true that the rich have taken only a little more than the poor. In fact, the rich have used far more of the carbon-absorbing properties of the planet than the poor have – perhaps ten to fifteen times more. There is a sense in which the poor really have been deprived of a resource. Smith is right to say that what is most precious is taken by the rich, but we are not talking about mere diamonds and gold. Burning fossil fuels, using the planet's sinks, has partly made developed countries what they are – it has been a large part of securing the standard of life enjoyed by those in wealthy countries. The resource which helped the developed world to do this is now effectively used up. In using the atmosphere as we have, we have not just consumed a little more than the poor. We've taken a possible future from them and replaced it with something much worse.

That might be enough for you. You might now be ready to conclude that the current distribution of the benefits and burdens associated with the use of the planet's carbon sinks is not just. The developed or high-income countries are using and have used much more than their share, and there are no morally relevant grounds for this inequality. Further, the poor are already enduring some of the costs of climate change in the form of extreme weather events, sea-level rise, food and water shortages and climate shifts. They've also missed out on a share of the sink, and there's a sense in which they've therefore missed out on better lives. These burdens are visited upon them through no fault or choice of their own. Certainly they have fewer resources which might be devoted to coping with climate change. Things are tough for them and easy for us because of an unfair distribution of a limited resource. Maybe more arguments will be forthcoming, but the traditional defences of private property are not persuasive in this connection. It's hard to find historical grounds which might excuse the current distribution of benefits and burdens. The distribution is therefore unjust.

So developed countries have a responsibility to do something: at the very least, we should begin to redress the balance by reducing our emissions. Given the present disparity between the emissions of developed and developing countries, the reduction will probably have to be dramatic. Probably the developed world should do something about the unpleasant future we have forced on the developing world too. The burden of proof for any claim that we might do otherwise, might continue to take more than their fair share, rests squarely with us.

You might also be willing to conclude that room should be made for developing countries to develop. However we come down in terms of targets or allocations – and we'll come to all of this in Chapter 5 – justice might demand that developing countries get a share of the sink if a share is going. If it turns out that emission allocations are highly restrictive, then justice might demand that developing countries get a larger share than developed ones. If anyone gets a seat at the table, they get a bite before we go back for seconds and thirds.

Maybe you will go so far as to think that corrective justice places further demands on the biggest fossil-fuel users. As we noticed a moment ago, if it turns out that someone has been sneaking extra shares of water from the well, compensatory or corrective justice might demand that he give water back or take less in the future. These sorts of thoughts might also lead you to the conclusion that developed countries ought to have a smaller share of the sink than developing countries. Other sorts of compensation might be due as well, particularly if you think a little about the suffering our history of fossil-fuel use has caused and will cause. The developed world might be morally obliged to pay for some sea-walls in Bangladesh, and a lot more besides.

If you are not ready to come to these conclusions just yet, one other, positive consideration might nudge you in their direction. Consider the following principle.

There is the thought that polluters should pay for the cost of their pollution. The thought has a history, going back at least to the 1970s, when certain European governments concluded that industries, not taxpayers, should pay for cleaning up such things as oil spills and the particular sorts of contamination which sometimes result from mining. The Polluter Pays Principle, as it is called, is embedded in the law of several countries, as well as the thinking underpinning at least some international agreements. The Rio Declaration on Environment and Development, for example, states that: 'National authorities should endeavour to promote the internalization of environmental costs and the use of economic instruments, taking into account the approach that the polluter should, in principle, bear the cost of pollution'.[14]

The principle is interpreted in different but related ways. Suppose that refining oil results in a hideous sludge which requires careful disposal. Some argue that the cost of coping with the goop ought to be born entirely by the producers of oil. Others claim that the users of oil bear some responsibility in these matters, and so the purchase price of oil products should include some portion of the cost of cleaning up. Other charges might be imposed by the government on a business if certain sludge reduction targets are not met. Perhaps a company has to put aside some money before it is permitted to drill for oil, money earmarked for dealing with the sludge. However you slice things up, though, it's clear that we have at least some basis in law for thinking about the relationship between environmental damage and responsibility.

The principle is based on something else, a deep part of our moral outlook, possibly a part of the bedrock mentioned in the last chapter or at least a thought deep down in the depths of morality. It has a lot to do with something else we glanced at a moment ago, namely the conceptual connection between moral and causal responsibility. This deeper principle is enshrined not just in law, but on posters taped to the walls of innumerable antique shops: 'If you broke it, you bought it.'

It hardly bears spelling out. You know exactly what I mean by it. The only real question in this connection concerns the identification of who is causally responsible for our 'broken' climate. If that's too rich for you, then the question is about who has causal responsibility for the bulk of greenhouse-gas emissions. The answer, undeniably, is the developed world. Singer, perhaps sighing audibly, concludes:

> To put it in terms a child could understand, as far as the atmosphere is concerned, the developed nations broke it. If we believe that people should contribute to fixing something in proportion to their

responsibility for breaking it, then the developed nations owe it to the rest of the world to fix the problem with the atmosphere.[15]

So reflection on historical principles issues in one clear conclusion: the developed world has a moral responsibility to take action on climate change. The question might be approached as a problem of distributive justice. The carbon sinks of our world are a finite resource which has been shared out unequally. Justice demands that we redress the balance. The question of responsibility might also be approached in terms of causal responsibility alone. Again, it is hard to escape the conclusion that the developed world has a moral responsibility to take action.

PRESENT ENTITLEMENTS AND CAPACITIES

It might have occurred to you to raise a few objections to the claim that history places moral demands on the developed world. Those objections might have something to do with intention or knowledge or even history itself. The objections can lead you to the conclusion that we should look away from history and focus instead on how things now stand. We'll start with the objections and then come around to the moral weight of present entitlements and capacities.

The concept of responsibility is something of a mixed bag, and we apply it in different directions. We sometimes have in mind causal responsibility, and when we do we refer to something insofar as it is a cause of something else. The rain, for example, can be causally responsible for the wetness of the garden. We also talk about legal and moral responsibility, and the rain does not stand a chance of being held responsible in either of these senses. The reason the rain is never held morally responsible for anything has a lot to do with the fact that the rain never knows or intends anything.

If you think I am morally responsible for some past action, say a lie, then at the very least you think I knew what I was doing. I knew the truth, but deliberately chose not to tell it. If you confront me, you might try to show that I had to know that what I said was false and that I had some reason for concealing the truth – maybe you found a motive for the lie, and you use that to uncover my real intentions. I might protest my innocence, claiming that I really thought that what I said was true. I wasn't lying at all. Maybe I can find a way to convince you that I came to believe some falsehood and innocently passed it on. You might be convinced that I didn't intend deception, that I didn't know the truth, and conclude that I'm not morally responsible for misleading you at all.

Couldn't a case be made for the claim that the developed countries did not know about the effects of greenhouse gases? Couldn't a case be made for the claim that they certainly did not intend to bring about climate change? If the developed world did not intend and did not know about climate change, then talk about historical principles of justice and responsibility for action sounds a little hollow. Perhaps we were too quick to conclude that the developed world has a responsibility to take action.

Consider first our knowledge of the effects of greenhouse gases. As we saw in Chapter 1, our understanding of the absorptive properties of atmospheric gases does not exactly depend on recent breakthroughs. Still, at least some philosophers and other thinkers who worry about knowledge and responsibility in this connection settle on 1990 as the year in which the world could no longer claim ignorance of the effects of emissions. Again as we noticed earlier, that was the year the IPCC published its first assessment report. Given the findings published there – data which got a lot of press – it is hard to forgive governments on the grounds of ignorance for their failure to act. If this sort of information has been widely known at least since 1990, it is hard to explain away our actions on the grounds of innocent intentions since that date as well. For what it's worth, greenhouse-gas emissions have been on the increase, by just about any measure you like, since 1990.

There are, anyway, certainly legal cases in which we do not shy away from holding someone responsible even though there are gaps in her knowledge. Many countries have plenty of distinctions in law which carve up the territory – conceptions of vicarious liability, strict liability, partial liability, diminished responsibility, manslaughter as opposed to murder, and so on. It is possible to think that some legal analogue might guide us in our thinking about climate change. Whatever the analogue might be, there's a good chance that we'll end up with the view that the developed world is responsible, maybe in some sense morally responsible for climate change, ignorant and innocently intentioned or not.

Perhaps we need not delve into the law to find a response to these objections. Suppose you bump into my car and cause a bit of damage. It's not my fault: I was legally parked at the time. Still, you bumped into me entirely accidentally – you neither knew nor should have known that you were going to hit my car, nor did you have any intention of doing so. Would it be wrong of you simply to drive off?

The question is not whether you would be legally wrong – probably you would be – but whether you would be morally wrong in just driving off. I'm inclined to think that you should pull over, maybe ask if I'm all right and try to help me if I'm not. If repairs are required on my car, I think probably you are stumping up something. Maybe the developed world has changed the climate entirely accidentally – it neither knew nor should have known that its emissions were doing damage, nor did it intend the damage. Wouldn't it nevertheless be wrong for the developed world simply to drive off, to leave everyone else on the planet in the lurch? Shouldn't the developed world pull over, make sure everyone else is all right, and pay for the damage? If not of all the damage, then maybe most of it? Some of it? Certainly we don't want to say that it owes nothing at all just because it neither knew about nor intended the damage.

There is one more objection in this neighbourhood, one more reason we might put aside historical grounds for responsibility concerning climate change, and it has something to do with the temporal smearing we glanced at in Chapter 2. Against the claim that rich nations ought to take action given their histories as green-house-gas emitters, one might take issue by saying that a lot of the damage was caused before most of the relevant nation's people were born. It smacks of original sin, you might be thinking, to say that I'm responsible for the ecological transgressions of my father. I didn't do it. He did. Maybe I'm responsible for my own minute emissions but not for the historical emissions of my country.

In order to get this objection up and running, I had to shift from talk of a government and its responsibilities to talk of individual people and their responsibilities. There are many such shifts in just about any discussion of the moral dimension of climate change. We both know that it's a mistake to assume that nations can have just the same properties as individual people. Still, we can and do talk intelligibly about a state's actions, intentions and desires, but from time to time we need to be as sure as we can be that we're not falling into some sort of mistake in talking and thinking in this way. If we are talking only about the actions and responsibilities of states, then probably there's not much room for saying that the state now is not responsible for the actions of the very same state one or two hundred years ago. No original sin there.

Even if we do admit that there is something to the claim that it is unfair to hold grandchildren responsible for the actions of their grandparents, the objection only gets going if we assume that the actions of the grandparents have nothing to do with the lives of the grandchildren. If my grandmother went in for a bit of car-jacking in her day, it would be wrong to hold me responsible for it. I had nothing at all to do with her actions, and her actions have nothing at all to do with my life as it now stands. But the case of climate change is more complicated than this. As Shue argues, the people alive today in the developed world are the beneficiaries of the industrial activities of their grandparents.[16] It's not true that their past activities have nothing to do with our lives at present. The stuff and the education and the medical care and, in general, the standard of living we enjoy is largely owed to the industrial activities of those who came before us. We benefit from those historical emissions, the same emissions which are partly causally responsible for climate change. The benefits we enjoy are causally linked to the suffering of others, both now and in the future. Are we not then morally obliged to do something about it?

I'll stop there, but it should be clear to you that these replies might be developed further. We might not be able to look away from history, but suppose, for the sake of argument, that somehow we manage it. Some are convinced that looking away is precisely what we'll have to do if we stand a chance of talking the largest polluters into coming to the negotiating table. Can we come to any conclusions concerning moral responsibility for action on climate change, just given things as they stand now?

We already know that present emissions are anything but equal. There are different ways of thinking about inequality and what to do about it, but if we think that fairness demands that a finite and precious resource be distributed equally unless we have morally relevant criteria for departing from equality, then we end up with the same conclusions now as we did when we took the history of our emissions into account. We end up with the view that the industrialized world has a responsibility to reduce its emissions.

Some just start with the default notion that everyone on the planet is equally entitled to a share of the sink. We'll come around to the details in Chapter 5, but for now we can at least notice that the rationale for such proposals need not be backward- or forward-looking. One can begin reflection on climate change by noticing that some nations currently burn more fossil fuels and therefore use more of the planet's limited absorptive resources than others. If we think that everyone is entitled to an equal share of what's going, all things being equal as it were, then the countries using more are the ones who ought to act immediately. It's the rich nations, on this view, who should aim for equality by cutting back.

The point might be strengthened by reflecting not just on emissions entitlements, but also on the varying capacities of rich and poor nations. You can approach these capacities from two different directions. First, there is a sense in which richer nations have more room for reduction, and second there is a sense in which richer nations have a greater ability to pay for reduction.

Consider room for reduction. Not all emissions have the same standing. It might make sense to think of some emissions as having more or different value than others, even if the quantity of emissions is just the same. The emissions resulting from the efforts of a farmer in Africa as he attempts to feed his family are not on a par with the emissions resulting from the efforts of an American dermatologist as he attempts to get to Vegas for a weekend of gambling. There is a meaningful distinction between subsistence emissions and luxury emissions, even if pinning it down takes some doing.[17] If it turns out that there should be some sort of planetary limit on emissions, then you might think that everyone ought to be entitled to emit enough greenhouse gases as required for subsistence. Maybe those emissions are non-negotiable. If subsistence emissions fall under the planetary limit, and we still have reductions to make, then we can only discuss reductions to luxury emissions. It's clear that developed countries emit a lot more of those than developing countries. Suppose that 50 per cent of the emissions of the US Virgin Islands are luxury emissions and all of the emissions of Rwanda are subsistence emissions. It's clear who has room for reduction and who doesn't. Arguing the point is as good as saying that some Rwandans should die so that some Virgin Islanders can recharge their mobile phones.

Consider the ability to pay for reduction. There are arguments here – disputes about how much switching to green energy will cost, what savings there will be from more efficient energy use, how much investment in new technologies will cost, how much it will cost a society to move its workforce from some sectors to others, and on and on. However all of this turns out, it's clear that reduction will cost something. There are other costs too. Philosophers and others distinguish between costs associated with doing something about emissions, so-called 'mitigation costs', and the expenses associated with coping with changes to our climate, so-called 'adaptation costs'. If we ignore history and think just about present capacities, a case might be made for the view that the richer countries ought to foot most of the bills.

Shue makes the point by comparing flat rates of payment to progressive rates of payment. Suppose three of us have to contribute to some common goal. I've got £100, you have £10, and Bob has £1. You argue for something which looks, on the face of it, as fair as can be: a flat rate of 10 per cent across the board as our contribution to the goal. I pay £10, you pay £1 and Bob puts in 10 pence. While this appears fair, it might well bankrupt Bob. Maybe the total amounts we started with are our annual wages, and it costs at minimum a pound per year to live. You and I comfortably clear the minimum level required for subsistence, but Bob is doomed. The money is small change to me, but it's life or death for Bob. Although the flat rate looks fair, what we are asking of Bob is too much. Maybe what we should have done was take our varying abilities to pay into account. The greater a party's assets, the greater the rate at which the party should contribute to the cause, or so one might conclude.

For Shue, the thinking underpinning this conclusion is enshrined in a principle of equity: 'Among a number of parties, all of whom are bound to contribute to some common endeavour, the parties who have the most resources normally should contribute the most to the endeavour.'[18] I suspect that the thinking here goes even deeper than talk of contributions and common endeavours. It has something to do with a moral principle which might be stated as follows: the better placed an individual is to do what is right, the greater the onus on him to do what is right. If you see a child drowning in the Thames, you've got some explaining to do if you don't try to save her. You have a lot more explaining to do if you don't try to save her and you happen to be a well-trained and physically fit lifeguard.

These thoughts can nudge you towards a final thought in this connection. Not only do wealthy nations have more room to cut back on emissions and a greater ability to pay for the necessary changes than poorer countries, they also have much more besides. Compared to the poor, the people who live in wealthy countries are formally educated for longer, the technological options available to them are greater, their countries' infrastructures are better, their capacities to produce and store food are more impressive, their access to quality healthcare is easier, their housing is better, and so on. In short, developed countries have the resources to do rather a lot when it comes to dealing with climate change. They are presently best placed for action by just about any measure you like. To garble Kant, sometimes, can implies ought.

SUSTAINABILITY

There are lots of ways in to reflection on sustainability. Here's just one.[19] Think about seeing the child in the Thames again. It doesn't take much reflection to conclude that you ought to wade in and save the child, even if it means some small cost to you, like getting your clothes muddy. You can have your own reasons for coming to this conclusion, and whatever they are, it probably won't matter much to you if the drowning child is right in front of you or a thousand miles away in Africa. Your proximity to the child in danger of death seems irrelevant to whether or not you ought to try to help. If you think you ought to wade in at some cost to yourself to save the child in front of you, it's hard to see how you might avoid at least writing a cheque to Oxfam in an effort to save a child some distance away. The point, for us, is that distance does not make a moral difference to what you ought to do. Both children matter. You can help them both. The fact that one is some miles away from you is not morally relevant.

Although I have no doubt that distance does not matter to morality, I also know that our responses are a lot more complicated than what reason demands. If proximity does not make a moral difference, it makes some sort of difference. It's a difference Weil notices and expresses well:

> Anybody who is in our vicinity exercises a certain power over us by his very presence, and a power not exercised by him alone, that is the power of halting, repressing, modifying each movement that our body sketches out. If we step aside for a passer-by on the road, it is not the same thing as stepping aside to avoid a bill-board.[20]

Proximity matters somehow. It matters when we walk down the street, and it matters even more when we walk past that drowning child. Seeing someone in distress, right there before our eyes, tugs heart-strings, moves us in a way that just knowing about distant distress, even seeing it on the evening news, might not. Even if we know something of this strange fact about us, it still does not budge the conviction that distance does not matter when it comes to what we ought to do. Hume knew that our moral instincts, which might get us going when we are directly confronted by some outrage or other, are matched by a sense of obligation which arises from reflection on what we ought to do in other cases. We can have this sense of obligation without the instinctive moral reaction, and maybe that accounts for the difference in our responses to the drowning child and the distant starving one. But, again, the difference is not a moral one: we know we ought to do something in both cases.

If spatial distance does not make a moral difference, it is hard to see how temporal distance could matter to what we ought to do. It might be thought that temporal distance brings more unknowns with it than spatial distance, and that somehow this excuses us from having duties to those in the future. I'm not so sure. We might not know the names of those distant people in Africa who we ought to help, we might not know if our cash or food will get through, we might not even know much about the precise effects of our efforts to help them, maybe we don't really know exactly what they will need or want most. None of this matters when it comes to the moral weight on us to do something about their lives. You might conclude that it cannot matter when it comes to the moral weight on us to do something about future lives.[21]

This way of thinking about sustainability might make it sound a little too close to charity. However, when we imagine wading in to save the child, what we are thinking about doesn't feel quite like charity. It feels like what we must do: at the least, a drowned child is a bad outcome to be avoided, even at considerable cost. You can feel the same way about a starving child in Africa and think that what you are doing is not exactly charity, but something which depends on a deeper sort of obligation – it's not a supererogatory act of kindness, but a morally required act. The same can be true of efforts to ensure a sustainable future.

There has been considerable recent reflection on the nature of sustainability, particularly as worries about the environment have worked their way up various agendas. It's not difficult to see that the concept depends on the notion that whatever resources are used, enough are left not just for future use, but for perpetual or indefinite future use. It's been said that sustainable living or development amounts to living on the Earth's income, not its capital, and there is certainly something to this fairly straightforward way of thinking. Probably the most influential formulation comes from the Brundtland Report to the UN: sustainability 'implies meeting the needs of the present without compromising the ability of future generations to meet their own needs'.[22]

The motivations for commitments to sustainability usually do not depend on talk of the irrelevance of distance to moral reflection. Instead, sometimes there is the claim that present humans do not have the right to deprive future humans of this or that, but talk of rights – particularly the rights of future people – can get you into trouble. There is also talk of stewardship, which I don't quite buy either, just because I have trouble seeing our recent arrival on the planet as mattering much to the planet's long-term prospects. I don't see why a primate, recently down from the trees, gets to be in charge.

Better motivations have more to do with the quality of future lives, even the bare existence of future people. The quality of future lives depends rather a lot on the world we leave in our wake. You can think about our use of other resources too, but focus on our use of fossil fuels. We know that continuing to use them at present or increased rates might result in a particularly horrible sort of world – a planet with more extreme weather, rising sea levels, trouble with crops and fresh water, floods, and on and on, maybe even a virtually uninhabitable world. You don't have to think hard to conclude that if future lives ought to matter to us, whoever they might be, then the world we leave to them ought to matter too. It might not be going too far to say that some of the societal actions we might take now, actions which are not sustainable, would result in the preventable deaths of a great many people, still more environmental refugees, disease, malnutrition, starvation, wars and suffering of other kinds. Avoiding all of that unnecessary pain through sustainable choices has a lot of moral weight behind it. It seems easy enough to see it.

What's hard to look square in the eye is the question of who ought to be bound by the demands of sustainability. It has been a little easy to point to the rich nations of the world and say that reflection on historical principles of justice or present capacities issues in the clear conclusion that they must take action on climate change. The action in question, it seems obvious, has a lot to do with cutting back, reducing emissions, maybe tightening belts, possibly paying for adaptation in the poorer parts of the world. We are now faced with the uncomfortable possibility that the poor nations of the world might have some belt tightening ahead of them, too. The demands of sustainability might fall upon us all equally. We've all got to think about those bad lives ahead.

Is the suggestion really that developing countries ought to be guided by concerns for a sustainable future, even if this means making large changes to present lives, lives which are only just getting tolerable, only just getting clear of poverty? And what about lives still lived on the edge? Can a country with a lot of starving people of its own to worry about really be expected to concern itself with the possibility of people starving in the future? There is something more than awful in all of this. At least some have thought that there's worse in here too, and it has already been claimed that the rich and powerful countries of the world will use talk of climate change as an excuse to stop the developing world developing, to keep the poor in check.

There are more upbeat voices who express the hope that the developed world will see to it that the developing world will leapfrog the worst of industrialization and join the rest of us living sustainable lives. On bad mornings you can have doubts about this hope. On just about any morning, however you find a way to think about it, sustainability seems to demand something from every one of us. The moral weight of all of those miserable future lives can seem crushing.

4 Doing Nothing

We all sorely complain of the shortness of time, and yet have much more than we know what to do with. Our lives are either spent in doing nothing at all, or in doing nothing to the purpose, or in doing nothing that we ought to do. We are always complaining that our days are few, and acting as though there would be no end of them.

Seneca

The last chapter might have convinced you that action on climate change is morally required. In particular, there's a lot of moral weight on the shoulders of developed or rich countries, and there's considerable pressure on the developing world to take action too. To think again about just a part of the argument, the developed world has used and continues to use an enormously disproportionate share of the carbon sinks of the world. Some of the premises on the table already can lead you from this fact to the preliminary conclusion that fairly drastic emissions cuts are necessary, requiring enormous changes in the way our societies generate and use energy. Before we get carried away, though, there might be good reasons for delaying or avoiding serious action, maybe just taking minimal steps, or possibly doing nothing. In this chapter, we'll have a look at some of the reasons offered for doing little or nothing at all.

UNCERTAINTY

Many of the world's biggest polluters have grounded inaction in reasons having to do with uncertainty in the science of climate change. In a prepared statement outlining the administration's reasons for failing to ratify the Kyoto Protocol, George W. Bush maintains that 'we do not know how much effect natural fluctuations in climate may have had on warming. We do not know how much our climate could, or will change in the future. We do not know how fast change will occur, or even how some of our actions could impact it.'[1] Uncertainty might be the most common reason offered for doing little or nothing about climate change.

Here is a way in to worrying about this sort of uncertainty. Doing something about climate change is going to involve some costs. Maybe it will cost a lot. If a nation commits resources to dealing with climate change, then obviously it is making a number of choices, going down one path and not another. Think just about the choices that matter most to many people, namely the economic ones. Money spent on, say, moving away from fossil fuels is money not spent on other things, like education, roads, housing and defence. These things make a difference in the lives of people, the lives of voters, and they can seem much more real and pressing than the distant threat of a few extra centimetres of sea level. Worse, what if we are wrong about climate change? What if we end up wasting money which might have been well spent?

It is easy to fall into these worries, and it is probably a lot easier if you are a policy maker who wants to keep her job, who has to explain her choices to people who want a piece of her government's spending. It matters to officials who want more than a job, who want to do what's best or right. Before money follows a problem, you could reasonably think if you were in her shoes, you have to be sure it's a problem and you have to be sure that you know what to do about it. We'll leave some other uncertainties – those having to do with economics as such – for the next section. What's needed now is certainty or at least high confidence in the science of climate change, but we are talking about the weather. We don't know for sure if it's going to rain tomorrow, so how can we possibly know about flooding in 2050? Is this sort of thinking well-grounded? Is Bush right to claim that we do not know how much effect natural fluctuations in climate have had on warming, how much our climate will change or how fast change will occur? More importantly, is this sort of uncertainty grounds for doing little or nothing?

You have heard a lot about what we know in Chapter 1. In particular, you have heard that the greenhouse effect is well understood. We also know that we are increasing the amount of greenhouse gases in the atmosphere by burning fossil fuels and using the land in certain ways. We know that this is making the planet warmer – we can expect between 1.1 and 6.4 degrees of warming in this century. We know that a warmer planet will bring with it heat waves, extremes of weather, new zones for the transmission of disease, changes to crops and the availability of water and so on. It won't hurt to be a bit more specific.

The IPCC tells us that the warming of the climate system is 'unequivocal'.[2] It has 'very high confidence' that the globally averaged net effect of human activities since 1750 has been one of warming'. Helpfully, the IPCC tells us exactly what it means by 'very high confidence': at least a 9 out of 10 chance of being correct. It is 'virtually certain' (which it defines as having more than 99 per cent probability of occurrence) that our future will be characterized by warmer and fewer cold days and nights over most land areas, as well as warmer and more frequent hot days and nights. It is very likely (more than 90 per cent probability of occurrence) that heat waves and heavy precipitation events will increase in frequency. It is likely (more than 66 per cent probability of occurrence) that the area affected by droughts will increase, as well as the intensity of typhoons and hurricanes. Increases in the amount of precipitation are very likely (more than 90 per cent probability) in high-latitudes, and decreases are very likely in subtropical land areas.

These projections are just for the present century. Beyond that, things really do get a little murky. For example, the IPCC says that it is very unlikely (less than 10 per cent probability of occurrence) that the deep ocean currents, like the Gulf Stream, will undergo an abrupt change before 2100. You can flip the statistic around and frighten yourself with the thought that, so far as we can tell, there's a 10 per cent probability that our activities actually will result in an 'abrupt transition' in our century. It is, however, very likely (more than a 90 per cent probability) that the circulation in the Atlantic will only slow down in the short term. Longer-term changes, though, cannot be assessed with confidence. Do bear in mind that we are now reflecting on the flow of ocean currents which keeps England and Europe generally a green and pleasant land – at least a more clement land than other places of the same latitude, like Greenland. It seems nearly certain that our activities are changing this, but there is uncertainty too: we don't know how dramatic the change will be or how soon the drama will come. If that is not unsettling, then maybe the following uncertainty is.

After 2100, the melting of the Greenland ice sheet and its contribution to sea-level rise might well become very worrying to an enormous chunk of humanity. If temperatures increase by anywhere between 1.9 and 4.6 degrees compared to pre-industrial levels – and they look set to do so according to many models – and if this increase is sustained for long enough, then Greenland will melt entirely. This would add another 7 metres to sea level. That's enough to swamp whatever low-lying areas you care to mention: vast and heavily populated tracts of China, India, Bangladesh, Egypt, probably all of The Netherlands, as well as cities like New York, Washington, Tokyo and London. There is uncertainty here – we don't really know whether Greenland will melt entirely – but the uncertainty makes me nervous.

There is a sense in which uncertainties like those associated with the prospects for the Gulf Stream and Greenland's ice can make you more inclined to action on climate change, not less.

When there's so much to lose, you don't need to be entirely certain to take preventative action, do you?

The IPCC admits to plenty of shorter-term uncertainties too. We do not fully understand what the carbon sinks of the world are up to, nor is the influence of clouds on the magnitude of climate change transparent to us. We only partially understand the effects of the oceans and the ice sheets on our climate. The dreaded positive feedback mechanisms themselves are only slowly coming into view. We understand all of this better as time goes on, but, worryingly, the more we know the more we revise our estimates of temperature increases upwards and timescales downwards.

It's important to understand just where the uncertainty lies. The many things we still don't understand all that well, the IPCC and others stress in various ways, make us unsure of the timing and the magnitude and the regional patterns of climate change. What is not in doubt is the fact of climate change and the human role in it. We know we are warming the world and we know how we are doing it. We aren't sure exactly how hot it will get or how quickly it will heat up, nor can we say just where the deserts, droughts, floods, fires, crop failures and refugees will be. There is a lot we cannot be certain of at present, but, the IPCC warns darkly, we also 'cannot rule out surprises'. We don't know what will happen to things like Greenland and the Gulf Stream.

Think again of that policy maker who frets about spending. There are at least two aspects of her uncertainty. She needs to be certain that there is a problem, and she needs to know what to do about it. There is no room at all for uncertainty about the existence of the problem of climate change. The seriousness of the problem is not in question either. Do we know what to do about it? We have at least the clear outlines of an answer: we should try to head off the worst of the possible changes to our climate by reducing greenhouse-gas emissions now, and we should prepare as best we can for the changes which have already been set in motion. The uncertainty, really, concerns only the timing and extent of the required cuts and preparations. We do not know how swift the changes to our societies need to be or how large they need to be. We don't know how much longer we can get away with the high-energy lives we've got. Maybe putting it that way makes our to-ing and fro-ing about action on climate change sound self-interested. Maybe that's just what it is.

Look away from that nauseating thought and focus your attention on the uncertainty we face. We know there are dangers ahead, but we don't know exactly what to do or exactly when to do it. Is this sort of uncertainty grounds for doing little or nothing? It helps to imagine an easier but similar case. Suppose you are considering the purchase of a house with a fine cliff-top view. You have heard about coastal erosion and decide to have a survey done. The survey tells you that the rate of erosion has been fairly slow over the past 100 years, but there is reason to think that its pace is increasing. Eventually the house will have to be abandoned – maybe in 50 or 100 years or, just maybe, sooner than that. You can't help thinking that it's a fine view. You make a few bad jokes about 'living on the edge' and buy the place anyway. You do take out insurance, however, and make sure that the place is covered just in case the worst happens. You were right to have the survey done. You are right to take out insurance.

When confronted with this sort of uncertainty – uncertainty which isn't about the fact of some future disaster but concerns what to do about it now – the right thing to do is to take precautions. This kind of uncertainty is grounds for taking action, not a reason for doing nothing. It would be odd to hear a person say, 'I know the house will fall over the cliff eventually, but I'm not sure when. So I'm not going to do anything about it.' You might sit such a person down and talk to him, very slowly. Maybe you should consider shaking him a little.

There are lots of variables which come into play when we make decisions in the face of uncertainty. The amount of uncertainty, obviously, makes a difference. If there were only a very small chance that the cliff might erode, then our conclusions about buying the place as well as buying insurance might have been different. The level of danger matters too. If we were worried about something less dramatic than the house falling over a cliff – maybe we are just concerned about the prospects for an outlying tool shed – then our thoughts about what to do might change. Sometimes our decisions are pressing, and this fact alone can force us into action in the face of uncertainty. Maybe I'd like to learn more about the chances that the cliff face will erode, but I know there are other buyers sniffing around the place, so I act more quickly than I would have otherwise. Who we put at risk through our actions can matter as well. You might forgive me for moving into the house on my own – maybe I'm putting myself in danger, but I'm doing so with my eyes wide open. If I know the place is dangerous, and I quietly sell it on to an unsuspecting family, you would be right to condemn me for putting others at risk. Maybe you have an obligation to stop me.

Think about these variables and climate change. Probably we should not be put off by the amount of uncertainty concerning climate change. As we've just seen, there's plenty of certainty where it counts. Further, the sort of uncertainty seems to warrant action, not inaction. The level of possible danger, too, seems more than high enough to act on. If it's true that the demand for action ought to be in proportion to the level of danger, then thoughts about the sharp end of some projections should be enough to lead to action. It is also true that our decisions are pressing. The planet is already changing, and it will continue to change before we manage to dispose of every niggling uncertainty. It's clear that we'll have to act long before we see some of the effects of climate change if we hope to avoid them – it takes a while to implement societal changes, and it takes a while for those changes to make a difference to our world. Probably we cannot wait until the worst of it is breathing down our necks. Finally, continuing on the present course puts innocent people at risk. We already know that the fact that some of those people are far away and that others have not been born shouldn't make a moral difference to us.

These thoughts, though only rough and ready, jive with our everyday, pre-reflective conceptions of danger, risk, uncertainty and action. There's plenty of room for tightening all of this up, but what we have is enough for me to conclude that at least one kind of uncertainty cannot give us good grounds for doing nothing about climate change. Other sorts of uncertainties are possible, of course, and we'll come around to some of them in a moment. If these garden-variety thoughts about the sort of uncertainty under consideration are not enough for you, maybe you need the support of an upscale moral principle or two.

The precautionary principle guides a lot of thinking in this neighbourhood. Maybe it's rooted in something close to moral bedrock: the no-harm principle or the general injunction against knowingly hurting others, all things being equal. I shy away from the precautionary principle because I take it that the rough and ready stuff is enough to go on, and also because I'm still not quite sure how to interpret the many versions of the principle itself, to say nothing of the attending implications of the many versions. My caginess shouldn't stop you from thinking about it carefully or even accepting it, if you like.

The precautionary principle has many incarnations.[3] Dubious versions can seem to restrict more or less any action which stands even a small chance of having adverse effects. More plausible characterizations of the principle take it that when we do not fully understand the effects of some technology or practice, the burden of proof when it comes to safety falls on the advocates of the technology or practice in question. If I have some doubts about your genetically modified beans, it's up to you to assuage those doubts. Until then, we err on the side of caution and keep your bizarre beans out of the ground.

There's trouble with thinking even of this sketchy version of the principle. What if my doubts are unreasonable? If you modified the beans, probably you know a lot more than I do about the dangers associated with them. So why should my doubts count for so much more than your certainties? Then again, if you modified the beans, maybe you have an interest in seeing the technology behind them go ahead – maybe you're willing to ignore your own reasonable doubts. While we're on the subject, what counts as a reasonable doubt? You can take these points and nevertheless look away from them, hoping against hope for rationality on all sides of a debate. You can also look away from dubious versions of the principle and focus just on perhaps the most relevant version, given our purposes.

This is written into the Rio Declaration, agreed by over 160 nations at the Earth Summit in 1992:

> In order to protect the environment, the precautionary approach shall be widely applied by States according to their capabilities. Where there are threats to serious or irreversible damage, lack of full scientific certainty shall not be used as a reason for postponing cost-effective measures to prevent environmental degradation.

This way of putting the principle does at least a few things. It reminds us that we do not need to be fully certain about damage to the environment in order to act against its possibility. It also reminds us that it is possible to know that something serious should be done but have doubts about the particular nature of the serious action needed. Those doubts, that uncertainty, should not be confused with being uncertain about the necessity of action itself. The lack of certainty, in this sense, cannot be a good reason for postponing precautionary action.

COSTS

There are several thoughts associated with the conclusion that we should avoid action on climate change because the cost is prohibitive. It might be claimed, quite simply, that doing something about climate change would just cost too much. Therefore, we shouldn't do anything. Although simple-minded, the conclusion gets you where you live. This might be why Bush pointed to economic worries when opting out of Kyoto. As he put it: 'complying with those mandates would have a negative economic impact, with layoffs of workers and price increases for consumers'.[4] Prominent Australians have recently made just the same claim. Relieved of buzzers, bells and high-minded preludes, the argument just is that such and such a proposal for action on climate change must be rejected because it will do damage to the economy, result in job losses, maybe ruin our current wealth or standard of living.

Just as it stands, there is something vicious about this. In the last chapter, you heard a great deal about the moral requirements for action. Can those requirements be overridden by talk of expense? Would you forgive someone for avoiding a moral obligation because he thought that it might cost him too much? He'd rather not give up his holiday in Bermuda, so those childcare payments will have to wait. If you think a little about the causes and effects of climate change – our easy high-energy lives as compared to the suffering which greenhouse-gas emissions cause and will continue to cause – you can come to the conclusion that avoiding action on climate change just because it might be expensive amounts to harming other people for money. That's the vicious bit.

It is possible, though, to recognize the existence of moral obligations for action, but couple this, quite rightly, with the aim of ensuring that money is well spent. There are numerous treatments of the economics of climate change which use a variety of models and forecasting methods, and they can tug in at least two general directions.

Some issue in the conclusion that we ought not to spend much on climate change.[5] Perhaps the most famous as well as the most controversial claims in this connection are made by Lomborg. He argues that we might spend our money dealing with any of a number of social ills – HIV, malnutrition, trade barriers, poor drinking water, malaria and so on. Climate change is just one of the world's troubles. We can do a lot more good, he maintains, if we put our money towards tackling other things and devote a relatively small amount of funding to, say, the research and development of renewable resources. He claims, for example, that implementing the Kyoto Protocol would cost the world as much as £180 billion each year, and what we would get for that investment isn't much: only a small delay to the heating of the planet. Much less, around £80 billion each year, would give everyone in the developing world access to basic healthcare, education, water and sanitation. Doing something about climate change would cost us a lot, we wouldn't get much return for that cost in the form of future benefits to humanity, and we could spend the money better on other things, right now.

Other analyses, in particular those put forward in the Stern Review, issue in a very different conclusion: the benefits of strong, early action on climate change outweigh the costs considerably.[6] Doing nothing or anyway very little to curb greenhouse-gas emissions will, Stern argues, cost the world at least 5 per cent of global gross domestic product each year. If some of the worst case scenarios are realized, the cost could be as much as 20 per cent of global GDP. In individual terms, every person on the planet will be about a fifth poorer than she might otherwise have been unless we undertake effective action immediately. That's an average, of course, and it means some people could be much, much worse off. Memorably, Stern argues that the major economic and social disruptions ahead, if we fail to do enough, are 'on a scale similar to those associated with the great wars and economic depression of the first half of the 20th Century'. It's not difficult to think that things will be worse than even this. However, the cost associated with taking strong action to cut emissions could be limited to as little as 1 per cent of global GDP per year. That's still serious money, but spending it now could ensure not only that we avoid the worst, economically speaking, but also that our economies stand a chance of continuing to grow. Doing a lot right now will not just save us from disaster, but the investment will bring dividends.

The IPCC, for its part, notes that a review of the literature on the economics of climate change turns up large ranges for the social cost of carbon emissions in particular and a number of different economic variables in general.[7] This is largely due, it says, to 'differences in assumptions regarding climate sensitivity, response lags, the treatment of risk and equity, economic and non-economic impacts, the inclusion of potentially catastrophic losses and discount rates'. In other words, the various models operative in economic analyses of climate change depend on a large number of assumptions, and the ones you make can have a dramatic effect on what your model says and, ultimately, what you think about the costs of proposals to deal with climate change. Valuations involve value judgements, and it nearly goes without saying that reasonable people can disagree about such things.

While there is certainty associated with some aspects of climate change, there is considerable uncertainty in the science where it counts for economic assessments: namely, it's hard to say just where and when the trouble will be regionally. Accurately quantifying uncertain damages is not easy. Maybe it's not possible. It is also hard to evaluate irreversible planetary damages. How might one begin to put a dollar value on the loss of whole species or ecosystems or people? How much is the Antarctic ice sheet worth to you? You can muddy the waters for yourself, if you like, by noticing that not everyone will agree about how much, say, a rainforest matters. This disagreement is not necessarily quantitative. Is my aesthetic valuation of it on a par with a local's view of it as a valuable source of food and lumber? What about the value another local places on it as his spiritual home? How do we match this up with someone else's conception of it as a valuable carbon sink? You can make matters even worse by noticing that it's not just all of our valuations which must figure into our reflections. How much will that forest be worth to the next generation, or the next, or the next? All of these interests matter too.

These considerations can lead you to the conclusion that economic analyses depend on something further upstream, namely our thoughts about what matters to us – what it is that we value. This is to say something much more than that economic models cannot hope to take account of the complexities and uncertainties ahead. It's not to object to this or that discount rate or to the sensitivity of some model or other. Instead, the claim is that reflection on values generally is conceptually prior to reflection with economic or monetary values in hand. We need to come to conclusions about the former before we can even take a step with the latter.

If this or something like it is the right way to think about the costs of climate change, then it seems clear that our conclusions about action cannot depend on the cost of action alone. Our conclusions about the cost of action depend on our assumptions concerning how much certain things matter to us. Those assumptions, which ultimately have a huge effect on our economic picture of the world, are themselves outside of economics. It is questions about value which need to be asked, not questions about costs. Putting costs first and claiming that costs inform our conclusions about our values is to get things exactly backwards.

TECHNOLOGICAL RESCUE

Reflection on technology and action on climate change is usefully divided into two different sorts of claims or hopes. First, one might say that some future technology will somehow save us from the worst of climate change. No action is needed now, one might think, because we'll eventually find a technological solution. We always find technological solutions to our troubles. Why should the problem of climate change be so different or difficult to solve? Second, and with a slightly straighter face, one might say that the technology we've got will save us from the worst of climate change. Maybe we can avoid serious efforts now because enough windmills and solar cells and carbon-storage systems will cut our emissions for us while our lives go on much as they always have. We'll briefly think a little about both of these possibilities.

Many put a lot of faith in largely untested, sometimes unknown, technological innovation. The thought, which might strike you as wishful thinking rooted in science fiction, has a number of adherents. Worryingly, the US might be its loudest advocate.

To take one of several recent examples, a part of the US's response to an early draft of the IPCC's 2007 report on the mitigation of climate change argues that 'modifying solar radiance may be an important strategy if [the] mitigation of emissions fails. Doing the R&D [research and development] to estimate the consequences of applying such a strategy is important insurance that should be taken out. This is a very important possibility that should be considered.'[8] By 'modifying solar radiance', the author means a kind of geo-engineering or terraforming, in this case reflecting some sunlight back into space in order to achieve a reduction in the effects of climate change.

Some have argued that a giant reflective screen might be put into orbit. We might waft a million little silver balloons into the atmosphere to reflect the sun's rays. The prospect of delivering a huge quantity of sulphate droplets into the atmosphere by rocket-powered explosives in an effort to simulate the cooling effects of a massive volcanic eruption has been countenanced. The quotation above calls talk of geoengineering 'insurance' that we should have just in case we fail to act in time. Maybe something will come of all of this, and there is no harm in keeping our options open. Our question, though, is whether or not the hope that we'll one day have space mirrors and such is a good reason for not acting now, for doing little or nothing?

Try to ignore the deeply dubious thought that we just might get lucky. Someone, somewhere, might invent something which does something else and saves us from climate change. Somehow. Think just for a moment about more concrete possibilities, perhaps the chance that geoengineering will stop the planetary changes we have put in motion. Maybe we can return ourselves to the climate of our largely stable, water-coloured, pre-industrial world by tinkering with sunlight itself. Think about a million little silver balloons boldly nudging aside the clouds. Think also about our planet's fidgety regulatory systems, which are now apparently out of kilter or anyway behaving in a manner we don't fully understand. Will a million little balloons fix it?

The IPCC is dismissive: 'Geo-engineering options . . . remain largely speculative and unproven, and [carry] the risk of unknown side-effects.'[9] Maybe being dismissive is not enough. There's no harm in wishful thinking, unless it stops you from doing something effective when something effective needs to be done. When wishful thinking takes the place of recognizing moral responsibilities, like those outlined in the previous chapter, the harm becomes a moral mistake. The damage which might have been avoided becomes the wishful thinker's fault. There is a lot of damage ahead if we fail to act. Opting for wishful thinking instead of action when there is so much at stake is something more like moral recklessness.

Science fiction to one side, there is the thought that the technology we already have will save us from the worst of climate change. Part of the hope in this connection has to do with the belief that we can avoid at least some meaningful action now because the implementation of certain technologies, either in hand or just on the horizon, will cut emissions for us. We can keep our televisions on standby if we simply switch to solar power. This line of thinking dangerously underestimates the amount of action required just to implement the technology we have.

In a thought-provoking paper which received a lot of attention both inside and outside of academe, Pacala and Socolow argue that the technology now exists which could enable us to stabilize carbon emissions at present levels within 50 years.[10] Stabilizing at present levels is one target which may or may not be enough to save us from the kind of temperatures which could bring with them awful changes to our world. If stabilization were achieved, we might then have to worry about reducing carbon levels. Still, stabilization in the medium term is considered by many to be a goal well worth having. Before you get the champagne out, though, bear in mind that even stabilization requires a massive effort on a planetary scale.

Imagine a graph with rising amounts of carbon-dioxide emissions on the vertical axis and time on the horizontal one. If you chart the increase in emissions observed over time, you get a clear trend upwards. If a point representing our current emissions were plotted on the graph, two lines might be drawn from it representing two pathways: a straight, horizontal stabilization line, a path to a world where emissions are held at present levels; and a line continuing upwards, showing carbon levels if nothing is done to curb emissions. Close the figure and you have what Pacala and Socolow call 'a stabilization triangle'.

The task is to find 'stabilization wedges', strategies which save emissions and flatten out the current trend in the direction of stabilization. Each wedge prevents a billion metric tons of carbon per year from being emitted by the time we reach the middle of the century. At the time the paper was written, 2004, Socolow claimed that we were emitting around 7 billion metric tons each year and were on course to emit 14 billion metric tons each year by 2054. It follows that 7 wedges are needed for stabilization. Pacala and Socolow identify 15 wedges. This stabilization strategy, this way of thinking about possible technological solutions, Socolow says, 'decomposes a heroic challenge into a limited set of monumental tasks'.

Think about just the two best-known renewable sources of energy: wind and solar power.[11] Consider wind power first. To get one wedge out of windmills, the world would need 2 million 1 megawatt windmills, replacing our current reliance on an equivalent amount of energy generated by coal. We have about 40,000 such windmills, just 2 per cent of what's needed for the wedge. It's worth noting that in the UK getting a single wind farm up and running takes years of bureaucratic fussing – mostly because locals would rather not have unsightly turbines messing up the fine view. What about solar panels? By the middle of the century, we would need 700 times the current capacity for a single wedge. This would require panels covering about 2 million hectares or 7,700 square miles – a land mass about the size of New Jersey or Israel. If weather patterns shift by the middle of this century, will our millions of windmills and miles of solar panels even be in the right places?

What about carbon capture and storage, the touted process by which carbon dioxide is snagged during power production and prevented from getting into the atmosphere? The technology is new, and there might be serious long-term troubles associated with it, but to achieve a wedge we would have to pump carbon dioxide into storage at about the same dizzy pace which we currently pump oil out of the ground. At present, only a handful of companies are experimenting with carbon capture and storage. Compare them to the huge number of facilities we have for sucking oil out of the Earth to get a grip on the huge effort required just for this wedge.

Could we be saved by biofuels? To get one wedge by around 2050, we would have to replace 2 billion of the fossil-fuel powered cars we would be driving by then with new vehicles running entirely on clean biofuels. These cars would also have to manage 60 miles per gallon, rather than 25 or so which is the current average. Supplying these cars with fuel would require the cultivation of 250 million hectares or about a million square miles of high-yield crops – roughly one-sixth of the world's cropland. There are growing fears that the race to produce biofuels is already leading to changes in land use which cause climate change – desperately poor farmers are burning rainforest for space to grow biofuel crops. In 50 years, when food crops are failing, growing seasons have shifted, droughts threaten, people are starving and on and on, will we really want to devote so much of whatever fertile land we have to feed cars rather than people?

There has been a lot of talk about hydrogen, the hydrogen economy and hydrogen fuel cells. The US has made much of the prospects for hydrogen, but at present hydrogen is not even an energy source – it takes more energy to produce hydrogen fuel than the fuel can deliver. Further, hydrogen is only as carbon-free as the energy source we use to produce it. The production processes available are costly, and the cheapest options at present result in carbon emissions. Storing the stuff isn't easy either. Because hydrogen happily exists as a gas, not a liquid, it requires a lot more space than petrol. The hydrogen fuel tanks on your new hydrogen-powered car might be considerably larger than the car you drive now. Storage problems could be solved by persuading hydrogen to exist as a liquid, but only at the cost of the energy required to get the stuff's temperature down to ridiculously low levels. Hydrogen might be a clean source of energy eventually, but, according to many estimates, we'll be waiting for about 50 years before we begin to see it. Promising, but it's no help to us right now.

You can come around to thinking that just about all of the technological 'solutions' on hand are like windmills, solar panels, biofuels and hydrogen: they are all certainly worth pursuing, but none can solve our problems for us. None of the possible paths look easy. The conclusion is not entirely pessimistic – certainly Socolow and his colleagues are not doom and gloom mongers. Their hope is to convince us that we need to pursue these technologies immediately if we are to do something meaningful by the middle of the century. At any rate, there is no reason at all to think that we can put off serious action in the hope that technology will rescue us. Just the opposite is true: Herculean efforts are required right now and for the foreseeable future if technology is to be of any help at all. What's clear is that we cannot go on as we are. We cannot reasonably cross our fingers, continue to build coal-burning power plants and drive SUVs, all the while thinking that technology will reduce our emissions for us. Probably what we have to do – in addition to enormous technological efforts like those scouted above – is change our lives. Instead of finding technological solutions for our energy needs, we have to find ways of needing less energy.

WAITING FOR OTHERS TO ACT

The claim that action on climate change should be postponed until others act takes a number of forms. Although an advocate of at least some action, Tony Blair has suggested that even if all of Britain's emissions were somehow instantly and magically stopped right now, in less than two years the growth in China's emissions alone would wipe out the difference. A reason given by Bush for opting out of Kyoto is that the agreement fails to make demands on countries like China and India. There are several thoughts worth disentangling here.

It certainly is true that some countries – China and India are the usual suspects – are developing at an astonishing rate. According to many estimates, China has already overtaken the United States as the world's biggest emitter of greenhouse gases. There are lots of ways to measure this sort of thing. It is worth pointing out that the US will continue to lead the world in per capita and cumulative emissions for quite some time, even in the face of explosive growth in the East. The average Chinese person is still responsible for much less than the average amount of emissions per capita on the planet – four or five times less than the emissions of the average American, and around two times less than the emissions of the average European.[12] Both India and China have rapidly expanding economies, growing middle classes with disposable incomes and human desires, and soaring energy demands. Both countries are also powered almost entirely by fossil fuels.

The first sort of worry to have about all of this, the Blair worry, can seem rooted in a kind of world-weariness: no matter what our efforts might be, the developing world's new emissions will simply swamp them. Say that the Kyoto savings on emissions will amount, in total, to around 500 million tons of greenhouse gases per annum by 2012.[13] By the same year, thanks to newly built, shiny coal-burning plants, India might well blot out the savings with around 500 million tons of brand new emissions each year. China could be emitting as much as 2,000 million tons of greenhouse gases from new power plants alone by 2012. If our efforts are more than cancelled out by their emissions, it's hard to see the point of our efforts.

The second worry to have, the Bush worry, might be rooted in a strangely blinkered conception of fairness. Some in the US have admitted that the US is responsible for a lot of the planet's annual emissions, but not all of them. Emissions are emissions, and the Earth does not care where they originate. Before the US does its share, it has to be sure that the rest of the world will do its share. Because Kyoto does not place restrictions on the emissions of some large developing countries, the US argues, it's a 'flawed treaty', and the US simply will not sign up. There's a kind of weird logic in this. It's not quite as careful as a prisoner with a dilemma. Instead, it can seem oddly reminiscent of the doublethink characteristic of *Catch 22*:

> ". . . Let somebody else get killed."
> "But suppose everybody on our side felt that way."
> "Then I'd certainly be a damned fool to feel any other way. Wouldn't I?"

If everyone else is emitting greenhouses gases without limit, then the US would be foolish to limit its own emissions. Wouldn't it?

One of the first things to notice in this connection is that both worries seem to miss the fact that the requirements for some sorts of action, particularly morally demanded action, are not contingent upon the action of others. If doing something is the right thing to do, it remains the right thing to do whether or not others are doing it too. If it's wrong, it's still wrong even if everyone does it.

Second, although it is true that sometimes it makes sense to refuse to act when others fail to pull their own weight, the case of climate change is different. I might, with reason, go on strike and leave my dirty dishes by the sink if my flatmates fail to tidy up after themselves. This failure to do what's normally required of me is ultimately self-defeating – eventually I'll have no clean plates for myself – but maybe my point will be taken, and my filthy friends will clean up after themselves. However, as Singer puts it:

> that is not the situation with climate change, in which the behavior of the industrialized nations has been more like that of a person who has left the kitchen tap running but refuses either to turn it off, or to mop

up the resulting flood, until you – who spilt an insignificant half-glass of water onto the floor – promise not to spill any more water.[14]

Singer's point, well-made, is that the industrialized world is not in the same position as a person refusing to act with good reason. The magnitude of the developed world's emissions is certainly a part of the difference. It's worth noting, too, that most of the industrialized world has at least agreed to start mopping up. The US's refusal to do so, against this backdrop, looks even more untenable.

You can ramp things up, put analogies to one side, and think seriously about the arguments for action, such as those considered in the previous chapter. The absorptive capacities of the planet are a scarce and precious resource. As Shue puts it, 'a huge store of ethical considerations that are irrelevant to unlimited supplies "lock in" when there turns out to be scarcity'.[15] It matters who uses how much of the planet's sinks, because one person's use effectively deprives someone else of a share. Further, the shares matter a lot: given the way our societies are set up, eating, drinking and generally continuing to live a life depends on emitting greenhouse gases. Shue's point, which needs to be taken as seriously as possible, is that ethical demands are placed upon the users of a scarce and valuable resource just because the scarce and valuable resource is being used. It does not matter whether a country signs a treaty, whether a country meant to deprive others, or whether other countries are pitching in too. The moral demand is there no matter what others do.

Maybe it's possible to have a little more time for the first worry, rooted as it is in world-weariness. You can end up with your head in your hands, more often than you'd like, when reflecting on what sometimes seems like the futility of actions to limit emissions. If you undertake any action, even a morally required action, you can legitimately wonder about the point if your good effects are cancelled out immediately. If you are a consequentialist – say a utilitarian who holds that the moral value of an act is determined entirely by its consequences for human happiness – then discovering that your act has no beneficial consequences is just to discover that your act is not morally required.

But the action undertaken by some countries right now will have beneficial consequences. Suppose 500 million tons of carbon dioxide are saved by the Kyoto Protocol. That 500 million tons is 500 million tons which were never emitted. It's 500 million tons off of the planetary total. Maybe, as some have argued, just taking steps in the right direction will make a significant difference in the future. Working towards saving those 500 million tons will teach us some lessons, perhaps make us better at saving the next 500 million tons. States might be expected to become more aware of the importance of action and take further steps – examples might be set for others. You might even try to peer through the confusing causal chains and think that saving 500 million tons of greenhouse gases saves future lives. These are all good effects which should figure into the calculations of any good utilitarian. I have doubts in this connection, and we'll get to them in the next chapter. Despite the doubts, the world-weariness can be given up.

URGENCY

We've just thought through the largest reasons given for delaying or refusing to act on climate change and found each one wanting. It would probably be wrong to find a single mistake in them, to try to reduce them all to just one sort of error of judgement. But there is something common to all of them, something which stands out a little if you look for it. Not one of the reasons for delaying mean-ingful action on climate change is based on a principle. Certainly there are no moral principles to be found in the arguments. There is not much talk of justice or equity or fairness or the value of human life. This fact might give you pause, might make you sus-picious, might make you wonder what the real motivation for delay might be.

We looked away, quickly, from viciousness and recklessness

when we found it in the arguments above. Maybe we should give it a little attention now. A part of the argument against action based on scientific uncertainty seems remarkable for its recklessness. Somewhere in there is the deluded thought that we can reasonably continue with our high-carbon lives because we do not really know when or where the ecological disasters will come. It amounts to a kind of gambling with the lives of people elsewhere on the planet now or in the future – betting that we can keep our comfy lives a little longer, while only risking their lives in the wager. There is a similar viciousness in the thought that the cost of mitigation and adaptation should be a reason for doing little or nothing. It amounts to harming others for money. The recklessness shows up again in the wishful thinking underpinning the hope for a technological quick fix. It's a ludicrous risk, a bet that we can continue with our lives as they are in the hope that something unknown or untested might make everything all right in the end. There is viciousness in refusing to act unless others do too. It is nothing less than ignoring the moral demands on us while simultaneously trying to place moral demands on others. Hypocrisy joins the list of our failures here.

It is hard to escape the conclusion that selfishness is at the bottom of the arguments against action. The arguments can seem appealing only if you operate with the premise that our lives matter more than the lives of certain others. If my life matters more than yours, then risking yours for mine in various ways can seem like a reasonable course of action.

Against the arguments for doing nothing is a further and perhaps final general consideration. Nearly every fact we have about the climate and the world and ourselves points to the urgency of action. Think just about the timescales involved. Carbon dioxide remains in the atmosphere and contributes to the effects of climate change for hundreds of years. Some of the planet's regulatory systems can move at, well, glacial speeds. Technological changes like the ones considered a moment ago will take decades to implement. Scaling back generally, changing the structure of the human world, probably won't happen overnight. A coal-burning power station built today will continue to do damage for its long operational life. The longer we delay – the more greenhouse gases we put in the atmosphere, the more forests we clear, the more damage we do – the more difficult it will be for us to reverse the processes we have set in motion. Some processes might not be reversible, but even slowing them down and thus giving us a better shot at adaptation is a goal worth having. The longer we delay, the worse our future will be. Any argument against action must somehow waft something more valuable than a better future for humanity in front of our noses. It is difficult to imagine what that something could possibly be.

5 Doing Something

It is not only for what we do that we are held responsible, but also for what we do not do.

Moliere

The last two chapters have shown that there is a moral demand for action on climate change and that there are no good reasons for avoiding it. Put simply, the governments of the world ought to do something meaningful about climate change. In this chapter, we will first consider what the world actually has done, then size up the moral case for two general kinds of proposal for what it should now do. It will help to have some criteria in hand, some standards we can use to judge the various proposals as well as the actions already undertaken. We'll have to get slightly technical, possibly a little high-minded, in this chapter, maybe stick closer to talk of criteria and proposals and historical facts than I might otherwise like. It might be rough sledging, but the pay-off is worth it. We'll end up with a clearer understanding of what action on climate change has been and ought to be.

Before we get underway, though, spare a moment for a brief fantasy. Imagine a world which took the 1990 reports of the IPCC very seriously. The governments of this world, acting prudently and in unison, immediately thrashed out mechanisms for eliminating greenhouse-gas emissions as quickly and as extensively as possible. The developed countries implemented and shared green technologies, cutting emissions and enabling the poor to leapfrog into cleaner economies; forests were protected everywhere, and new ones were planted; policies ensuring energy efficiency in transport and industry took effect; rich countries pitched in to help the poor of the planet adapt to the changes already set in motion. As much future suffering as could be avoided was avoided, and future generations looked back on this massive effort with a mixture of gratitude and something like awe.

This is just a fantasy. The point is that it could have happened but didn't. What future generations will make of us, given what we actually have done, almost does not bear contemplating. Thinking about their judgement, though, can focus our attention on the importance of being as careful as we can be to do what's morally right in the time we now have.

CRITERIA OF MORAL ADEQUACY

Proposals for action can be evaluated in a number of ways. Much depends on what you think matters most. It might be said that a proposal is adequate in practice, that is to say that it will get the job done given certain realities. Maybe a proposal is adequate given particular economic facts or principles: it's affordable or gives us good value for money. Proposals might be called other things besides – they might be efficient or workable, maybe manageable, even politically desirable or generally expedient. What interests us, though, is the moral adequacy of proposals for addressing climate change. Given our earlier reflections in Chapter 3, we can put three criteria on the table immediately. A morally adequate proposal must take due account of:

(1) historical responsibilities,
(2) present capacities, and
(3) sustainability.

To these we can add something new, (4) procedural fairness, which we will come to in a moment. The suggestion is that any proposal for action on climate change must at least satisfy each of these four moral requirements. Other moral demands are possible, but we can say with some confidence that a proposal is morally inadequate if fails to take any of these four things seriously. It won't hurt to think about each one for a moment.

First, there is a clear sense in which some countries bear more responsibility than others for our changing climate. It is a straightforward fact that some countries have emitted more greenhouse gases – used up more of the planet's sinks, caused more climate change – than others. It's a quantifiable fact: we know something about cumulative emissions. This fact can be coupled with a number of premises, of the sort already considered, and the result is the view that the burdens associated with adaptation and mitigation should be distributed in line with what we know about past emissions. Thoughts about justice, about the Polluter Pays Principle, the connections between causal and moral responsibility and so on, all issue in the thought that the developed world has extra duties, deeper responsibilities and more obligations – put it however you like – when it comes to action on climate change.

Second, we know that present emissions are unequal – again the developed, rich world is emitting far more than the developing world. I have per capita emissions in mind, but the developed world will still emit more than the more populous developing world by other measures for a while yet. Fairness, perhaps some conception of rights or equal entitlements, the importance of subsistence emissions, all of these things point towards the conclusion that a finite and precious resource should be distributed equally unless we have some morally relevant criteria for departing from equality. We also know something about the varying capacities of the rich and the poor on the planet. Both of these sets of facts about the present support the conclusion that the developed world should take on a proportionally much greater share of the burdens associated with adaptation and mitigation.

Third, there is something to be said for reflection on the rights of future people, stewardship or the general fact that the lives of future people ought to matter to us. The demands of sustainability fall upon all countries equally. If our interest now is in particular proposals for action, we need to consider sustainable levels of greenhouse-gas emissions, if there is such a thing. We have managed to avoid the particulars of our obligations to the future so far, but the rationale for morally adequate action on climate change will have to take them up in detail. In a sense it is this criterion which constrains the others. Only after a case has been made for the claim that some level of emissions or other is sustainable can we go on to talk about the just or fair division of those emissions. This case will depend on at least two things: our best scientific thinking about the climate; and our values, in particular, the value of lives to us.

You can spot the relevant empirical part of a proposal for action by looking for talk of targets for levels of greenhouse gases and temperature. Before the Industrial Revolution, carbon-dioxide levels were around 280 parts per million (ppm). Levels passed 380 ppm in 2005 and about 2 ppm are added each year. The rate of the rise is increasing too.[1] The relationship between carbon dioxide in the atmosphere and temperature is certainly worth knowing. A measure of the temperature increase associated with a new equilibrium state if the carbon dioxide in the atmosphere doubles as compared to pre-industrial levels is called 'climate sensitivity'. Coupled with measurements of the amount of carbon dioxide actually in the atmosphere, it can give us a sense of the timing of climate change, among other things. Efforts to calculate climate sensitivity therefore get a lot of attention. The best guess at present is in the range of 2 to 4.5 degrees.[2] Proposals for action will have to set specific targets in the light of all of this – perhaps in terms of upper limits to temperature increases or levels of carbon dioxide in the atmosphere – anchored in our clearest understanding of the climate. Other sorts of targets are possible too, but some sorts of precise aims are certainly required.[3]

There is no shortage of limits, targets and proposals. At present they seem to cluster around 60–80 per cent reductions of 1990 greenhouse-gas levels by the middle of the century. The UK government thinks it should aim to reduce its emissions to 60 per cent of 1990 levels by 2050. The Pew Center on Global Climate Change argues for cuts of 60 to 80 per cent by 2050.[4] The Global Commons Institute puts the upper limit of carbon dioxide at 450 ppm, arguing reductions of 80 per cent are needed by 2050.[5] The 2 degree limit is also mentioned in many calls for action at the moment. Certainly the IPCC maintains that increases in globally averaged temperatures above 1.5–2.5 degrees are associated with more rapid warming and more 'negative impacts'.[6]

Recent books have certainly latched on to the 2 degree limit too. Lynas argues that any temperature rise above 2 degrees triggers a feedback in the Earth's natural carbon cycle which puts more carbon dioxide in the air and pushes us past 3 degrees, which will melt permafrost and put enough methane in the atmosphere to get us past 4 degrees, which stands a good chance of releasing even more methane from the oceans, which pushes us past 5 degrees, which is more or less curtains for most life on Earth. This means, he argues, that global emissions have to peak no later than 2015 and fall off quickly thereafter, stabilizing at no more than 400 ppm.[7] It's a tall order. Monbiot argues that a monumental 90 per cent cut is required in the emissions output of industrial countries by 2030 – a staggering and swift change, although he goes on to argue that it is possible.[8] The hope again is partly to keep the change under 2 degrees.

Just what the targets should be is, obviously, a matter for further reflection at the moment, largely because we have only a partial grip on feedback mechanisms, sinks, clouds and such. However, there is no doubt that the cuts required are substantial and that they ought to be implemented as quickly as possible.

We may not know exactly where emissions levels should be, but it's clear that present levels are far too high. The scientific aspect of any proposal for action will only satisfy the sustainability criterion if it manages to make a compelling case for the cuts or targets it advocates, in line with our best understanding of the climate system.

The part of the proposal having to do with the value of lives is sometimes couched in terms of risk. The more emissions we allow, the warmer the world gets, and the larger the risk of danger to us and to those who come after us. The acceptable level of risk depends on lots of things, but certainly it depends largely on how much future people matter to us. If they don't matter, then we are not risking much by allowing emissions levels to rise. The part of the demand for sustainability having to do with value says that they ought to matter a lot, and at the very least proposals should assure us that the action advocated does not put them in unnecessary danger. What's acceptable or necessary, what's worth the risk and why, should be spelled out by the proposal in question. We should get a compelling justification for the values embedded in its conclusion.

Finally, morally adequate proposals must be the result of fair procedures. Different accounts of procedural justice or fairness require different things, but at minimum certain sorts of elements almost have to be in place before an agreement even stands a chance of being fair. All parties to the agreement should have an equal share in the information relevant to a decision and an adequate understanding of the facts. The process of arriving at agreement itself should be an open and transparent one. There should be a kind of freedom built into the process which ensures that no one is forced to consent. Certainly, parties lumped with burdens ought to know exactly what they are getting themselves into, and they ought to get themselves into it freely – obviously they have a fair say and participate fully in the proceedings. In short, no one takes advantage of anyone else; the wool is not pulled over anyone's eyes.

UNFCCC AND KYOTO

What has the world actually done about climate change? Given the criteria sketched above, have the efforts of governments been morally adequate?

In 1992, two years after the IPCC's first report, world leaders met in Rio de Janeiro for what came to be known as the Earth Summit. An agreement called 'The UN Framework Convention on Climate Change' (UNFCCC) was put on the table and eventually signed and ratified by nearly 200 countries. The principles operative in the convention are interesting and familiar.

For example, the UNFCCC begins by acknowledging the fact of climate change and the human role in it. Then, a third of the way down the first page, the convention explicitly recognizes that

> the largest share of historical and current global emissions of green-house gases has originated in developed countries, that per capital emissions in developing countries are still relatively low and that the share of global emissions originating in developing countries will grow to meet their social and developmental needs. . .[9]

This is impressive, in a way, because it amounts to the recognition of some of the premises which we needed in two arguments for the conclusion that the developed world has larger responsibilities for action on climate change than developing countries.

In fact, something very near this conclusion appears just a few lines down: climate change calls for co-operation and participation by all countries 'in accordance with their common but differentiated responsibilities and respective capabilities and their social and economic conditions'. It goes on, recognizing 'the need for developed countries to take immediate action'. The developed world 'should take the lead in combating climate change' while leaving room for the developing world to develop: 'their energy consumption will need to grow'. These points get made again in the document. It even builds in a version of the precautionary principle: 'The Parties should take precautionary measures to . . . minimize the causes of climate change and mitigate its adverse effects.' All of this seems to be on its way to meeting the first and second criteria of adequacy.

Even the third criterion is nearly met. The 'ultimate objective' of the UNFCCC is the

> stabilization of greenhouse gas concentrations in the atmosphere at a level that would prevent dangerous anthropogenic interference with the climate system. Such a level should be achieved within a time frame sufficient to allow ecosystems to adapt naturally to climate change, to ensure that food production is not threatened and to enable economic development to proceed in a sustainable manner.

The convention even delivers something of a specific target: countries should voluntarily aim to return to their 1990 levels of greenhouse-gas emissions. There is talk of sustainability too, as well as the importance of future generations, even if there is no specific justification for setting the targets themselves or an accompanying consideration of value.

The real trouble is that none of this is in any way mandatory or binding on the signatories. It's not easy to evaluate a proposal for action on moral grounds if the proposal does not actually commit countries to action. The treaty is only a framework on which hang certain principles. It does not tie any country to targets or deadlines but proposes to work towards such things in the future against a certain background. The UNFCCC's voluntary targets, by the way, did nothing much to curb emissions in the 1990s. By 2000, for example, US greenhouse-gas emissions were up by 14 per cent compared to 1990 levels.[10] Kyoto is the actual effort, the attempt to do something, to place binding targets on countries. Although the UNFCCC is on its way to meeting the criteria of moral adequacy, we'll have to have a look at the Kyoto Protocol if what interests us is the moral value of the world's efforts on climate change.

Since the ratification of the UNFCCC, there have been annual Conferences of the Parties of the Convention. The Kyoto Protocol was tabled at the third Conference in 1997. The mechanisms of the treaty are such that it could only come into force if it were ratified by at least 55 industrialized countries, including countries undergoing the process of transition to a market economy, together accounting for at least 55 per cent of the total greenhouse gas emissions for 1990. Australia and the US famously refused to ratify the treaty. Given the figure of 55 per cent and their enormous emissions, Kyoto nearly collapsed when they walked out. In 1997 the US Congress voted against ratifying anything produced by the UN which did not place binding emissions cuts on developing countries, and we have also seen that the Bush administration argued against Kyoto too. When Russia finally ratified the treaty, enough countries were on board, and Kyoto finally became law in February 2005.

Kyoto does several things. Importantly, it places specific emissions targets on participating countries. The overall goal is to reduce emissions by at least 5 per cent below 1990 levels of the countries taking part, and each country has its own target. For example, Japan is to aim for a 6 per cent reduction; many Eastern European countries have targets of 8 per cent; some countries, like Norway and Iceland, are permitted to increase emissions; other countries are expected to maintain 1990 levels. The EU decided to club together and aim for 8 per cent reductions as a unit, enabling some countries to miss their targets while others pick up the slack.

Kyoto sets a timetable too: targets must be reached between 2008 and 2012. It also allows for emissions trading: if a country misses its target, it can buy allowances from another country which is doing better than required. Developed countries can also earn emissions credits by paying for green projects in developing countries (the Clean Development Mechanism) or by helping another developed country reduce its emissions (the Joint Implementation Projects). All the while, the developing countries are expected to make preparations to join in future rounds of emissions cuts.

Ask yourself if all of this satisfies the criteria of moral adequacy. You might expect a morally adequate treaty to place heavy demands for emissions reductions on those most responsible for climate change, as well as further demands on those presently best-positioned to take action. Present emissions might be nudged nearer equality with additional reductions placed on those currently emitting most. The rationale for action would couple a scientific justification with a moral one, both of which take seriously the needs and lives of future people. The process underpinning the entire agreement would be a fair one.

Did Kyoto do some or any or all of this? Perhaps the best way to answer this question is to consider the targets specified by Kyoto. The individual targets themselves are not based on principles having to do with responsibility, entitlements, present capacities, or sustainability, but on what many have called 'horse trading'.

Before pulling out of the treaty entirely, the US and Australia fought hard to weaken the treaty. For example, rather than agree to reduce emissions outright, they lobbied to have their forests or forestry conservation projects count against their emissions targets.[11] In the end, concessions made to Australia would have enabled it to increase its emissions by 8 per cent had it ratified the treaty. The EU won the right to function as a single entity, with a joint emissions target of 8 per cent, no doubt knowing that this target would be all the easier with the inclusion of Eastern European countries whose emissions were falling in line with their troubled economies. After 1990, Russia's emissions also plummeted – below its 1990 levels – along with its fragmenting economy, and it seems likely that Russia signed up knowing it could make a lot of cash by trading emissions allowances to countries unable to reach their objectives so late in the day. The individual targets set for countries in Kyoto are based on self-interest, not moral principle, certainly not in the recognition of past injustices or present inequalities.

Add to this a little reflection on the sustainability requirement in both its scientific and moral aspects. The Kyoto Protocol offers no scientific or moral rationale for its 5 per cent target. The target is, anyway, not at all easy to justify on either sort of grounds. It is ludicrously small compared to the enormous cuts endorsed by just about any serious agency you like – as we have seen, cuts of 60 to 80 per cent on 1990 levels by 2050 is in line with plenty of thinking. Some say larger cuts are needed even before the middle of the century. The risk to human beings associated with Kyoto's small target suggests that concern for the value of life had little to do with its formulation. Even if you squint, it is difficult to see how the Kyoto target could make sense from any reasonable understanding of climate science or decent conception of the value of human life. The target is without scientific or moral justification.

Think now of the fourth criterion, the one having to do with procedural justice. It's clear that the procedures underpinning the agreement are wanting, not just or fair. I'm not thinking now of horse trading but of the fact that there were no measures to ensure the equality of the players in the process insofar as the process itself is concerned. Probably the wealthy, industrialized world recognized its many advantages and used them to secure further advantages – no doubt at the expense of weaker countries. The word 'bullying' has been used, and other words might occur to you. A process certainly cannot be called 'just' if those landed with large burdens have little say in the process. There is a sense in which the poor and the weak, those least able to adapt to climate change, were landed with the worst of the burdens: rising tides, drought, failing crops, more disease, water shortages, and on and on. That fact should have secured certain countries a much larger role in negotiations. It didn't.[12]

Hold on, you might think. Maybe Kyoto is morally lacking, but we have to start somewhere. It has been argued that a first step towards something worthwhile, even a tiny first step, is justification enough. Agreement was needed to get the required number of industrialized countries on board for Kyoto to come into force. We should look away from the moral failings underpinning that agreement, because the agreement is worth it. We now have a framework for emissions cuts. We have proved that it can be done, that the world can work together on climate change. Maybe the ends justify the means.[13]

There are a number of traditions which are willing to say that sometimes the ends justify the means. It is possible to excuse a morally dubious act if the act itself results in something worth having which couldn't have been had otherwise. The excuse, then, has two parts: the thing secured, the end, is worth having and the means is the only way to get it. Sometimes there is a third component: the means cannot be all that bad. No one thinks mass murder might be justified by some worthy end. Other components can be fitted in too.

To buy into this sort of view of Kyoto – that Kyoto is a means to an end worth having – at the very least you have to think that the desired end is now on the cards. You have to think that future rounds of deeper cuts with more industrialized countries taking part now stands a good chance of being a reality because of Kyoto. Further, you have to have good reasons for this thought; it can't just be wishful thinking. Otherwise Kyoto ends up being nothing more than a morally inadequate action undertaken in the barest hope that something good might come of it. You need more than hope if your excuse is to hold water. It also has to be true that your dubious means are the only way to secure the good end you want. It has to be true that Kyoto was the only way to secure the future good end of a meaningful treaty with substantial and binding emissions cuts. There is at least one other way to get such a treaty, and that's to start with it. Finally, you have to be sure that Kyoto is not that bad a thing, but it might be true that Kyoto amounts to nearly 20 years of merely gesturing towards meaningful cuts, and maybe this is a fairly enormous wrong – a large harm our governments are doing to present and future people. The governments of the world, you might conclude, could have done a lot better than they in fact did. Maybe in this case, the means just cannot be justified.

How might they have done better? What might the world do now? There are a number of possibilities.[14] We need to narrow the field.

We'll ignore a few straight away, given their obvious failure to satisfy the criteria of moral adequacy. Consider, for example, variations on the bold view that the status quo should be preserved.[15] One might argue that past usage confers something like the right to emit. So all countries might well have a reason to reduce emissions, but future allocations should be based on the present proportions of emissions by country. If Cuba is responsible for 1 per cent of present emissions, they ought to have 1 per cent of future emissions, whatever the global reduction might have to be. You might be able to talk yourself into this by thinking of squatters' rights or even a utilitarian muddle having to do with avoiding the pain caused by changing lives accustomed to cushions. You can talk yourself right out of it again by thinking about three things which override such considerations: historical responsibility, present capacities and future human lives. The pain of living without cushions, for example, gets trumped by the pain associated with starving to death.

We'll also ignore some suggestions which might be worth pursuing in other contexts. The criteria we have apply best to full-blown, comprehensive proposals for action on climate change, so that's what we'll consider. There are other things floating around too, policy suggestions and pitches for dealing with some specific part of negotiations on climate change.[16] Such things might be judged against a subset of the criteria for moral adequacy, or we might think it best to use them all.

We'll also look away from other proposals, mixed proposals which contain elements emphasizing more than one sort of approach.

We'll consider just two sorts of proposal, arguably two large types which encompass a lot of the proposals going. The first seems to satisfy the criteria of adequacy; the second doesn't but makes a case for not doing so. You can also think of these two types as emphasizing two things which might be of equal importance anyway: emissions entitlements as against the burdens associated with action on climate change. The contrast might help us to see the proposals more clearly, and also get us close to the centre of at least one large dilemma associated with climate-change negotiations. It might be the largest dilemma. I have no doubt that there are other proposals with moral criteria in mind, but we'll start with and stick to a consideration of equal per capita shares, as it seems to tick most of our boxes.[17]

EQUAL PER CAPITA SHARES

Probably the most obvious solution to the problem of emissions allocation is also the one most likely to jive with an ordinary sense of justice or fairness. Start with the truth that the planet's capacity to absorb greenhouse-gas emissions is limited. If there actually is a level of emissions which we think the planet can handle without unnecessary danger, then emissions corresponding to that level ought to be shared out equally. Everybody should have an equal slice of the planetary pie.

Singer, for example, argues that we might try just to stabilize emissions at present levels. At the time of writing, he maintains that this works out to about one metric ton of carbon emissions per person per year. 'This therefore becomes the basic equitable entitlement for every human being on this planet.'[18] Comparing this ration with actual per capita emissions, Singer goes on to show that countries in the developing world have room to grow, to increase emissions, as the current average there is around 0.6 tons per capita. China, for example, could increase emissions by as much as 33 per cent. The developed world, however, would need to make large cuts. The US would have to cut emissions to about one-fifth of its present levels.

Many wrinkles show up quickly, and they can lead to changes or additions to the equal per capita proposal. In Singer's version, the developing world might 'generously overlook the past' and agree to focus just on present per capita shares. In doing this, Singer aims to make the proposal at least slightly palatable to the governments of rich countries, and we'll come back to this thought in a moment. But if you are persuaded that the first criterion of moral adequacy matters, you might insist on historical responsibility playing some part. Singer himself thinks about this a little, arguing that taking into account some backward-looking principle, such as an historical principle of justice or the notion that polluters should pay for pollution, leaves the developed world with much less than equal per capita shares. Given the probability that dangerous anthropogenic climate change is already underway, it might well be that historical considerations issue in the conclusion that the developed world has already used up more than its share of the sinks. It is not entitled to further emissions at all.

Here we bump into a particularly difficult question. How can we translate differing sorts or amounts of responsibility into aspects of an equitable proposal for the allocation of emissions?[19] If we interpret historical demands in such a way that they can only be met by having a direct bearing on emissions allocations, then we might be left with something awful: the insistence that the developed world is not entitled even to subsistence emissions, that it is somehow right that people in the developed world die rather than use more of the planet's resources.[20] Maybe this is a *reductio* of at least some sorts of direct interpretations of historical responsibility. In other words, if direct interpretations issue in this intolerable conclusion, then there must be something wrong with them. What's needed, probably, is some sort of indirect linkage, and the usual suggestion has to do with money.

Here's a cartoon version for you. Perhaps a figure is put on the cost of mitigation strategies needed in the developing world, and the contributions of developed countries are based on their respective cumulative emissions somehow coupled with their present abilities to pay. Perhaps a fund is also set aside for disaster relief, housing, medical aid and so on which might go towards adaptation costs in the developing world. Again, probably contributions are in line with historical responsibility – maybe cumulative emissions totals translate into shares of the costs. The amounts of money involved would no doubt be enormous. In effect, a lot of the wealth accumulated by the rich countries on the back of greenhouse-gas emissions would now flow to poor countries, among them those who will suffer most as a result of the emissions themselves. It's an indirect linkage, but possibly a just one.

If you think a little about the second criterion for moral adequacy – the one concerned with present capacities – a number of practical problems with the per capita solution might occur to you. Probably people in different countries need emissions for different things. Some of this 'need' is bogus, but I have in mind needs like those associated with accidents of geography. Subsistence emissions, in other words, are not equal across the board. The average Norwegian might need more emissions shares than the average American, because Norway is colder in the winter, and without heat lots of people would freeze to death. Maybe emissions shares go further in a country which has the cash to spend on increased efficiency. It's also true that people in one country might use up emissions shares by producing things for people in another – sometimes one country produces and sells energy to another. Perhaps the cost associated with the emissions lost can be built into the final costs of goods.

Another practical wrinkle can show up just as quickly. If we agree that emissions allocations should be based on numbers of people, we effectively encourage something which compounds our problems on Earth: population growth. Solutions have been suggested; in particular, we might tie allocations to population figures for a specific time. Singer, for example, argues that per capita allocations should be based on estimates of a country's population in the future, to avoid penalizing countries with young populations. No matter how you come down on all of this, equal per capita allocations might not be as simple as they sound.

You might also encounter a theoretical problem in this connection, something associated with a duty to aid the least well-off. Rawls, for example, argues that we might have good grounds for departing from an equal distribution of resources if we hope to help the worst-off.[21] In fact, we might have a general duty to help the worst-off, and if you put a lot of weight behind it you might think that equal per capita shares of emissions, although apparently equitable, actually result in a kind of moral error. You might think that any distribution which leaves the rich rich and the poor poor cannot be justified, even an equal per capita distribution. Until other inequalities are addressed, opting for simply equal emissions allocations is itself somehow wrong.

To be sure, these wrinkles and worries are not knock-down objections. The equal per capita option is certainly a live possibility. One of the most attractive versions is called 'Contraction and Convergence' (C&C), and it rightly receives a lot of attention.[22] As the name suggests, C&C is a model with two parts. The governments of the world begin by reaching agreement on some particular greenhouse-gas target: some global limit to emissions and a date when this limit must be reached. C&C can then determine how quickly current emissions must contract in order to achieve the target. On the way to the target date, global emissions converge to equal per capita shares.

The moral adequacy of this particular proposal depends on how its parts are cashed out. The Global Commons Institute, the largest advocate of C&C, makes a point of emphasizing what we have been calling the sustainability criterion: the greenhouse-gas budget we opt for ought to be tied to our best current scientific thinking, and it ought to be extremely risk-adverse. A large emphasis is not placed on historical responsibility, but certainly C&C requires larger burdens for faster and more substantial reductions on the part of developed countries. It does satisfy at least a large part of the present capacities and entitlements criterion, most obviously because it aims towards equal per capita emissions, but also because it allows for emissions trading. Whatever else it might do, emissions trading tends to narrow the gap between the rich and the poor. Finally, C&C is at least a long way down the road to procedural fairness. Rooted as it is in the notion that everyone has equal access to the atmosphere, there's just no room for either horse trading or bullying. From a moral point of view, C&C has a great deal to recommend it.

COMPARABLE BURDENS

The thought that some concessions might be made to developed countries, just to get them on board, has already surfaced twice. We've seen it as a possible reply to the moral failings of Kyoto. Singer also suggests that developing countries might generously overlook the past, and it seems likely that selective attention of this sort is undertaken in the hope that the rich might agree to per capita shares. I've argued that this sort of thing does not excuse Kyoto, but nothing I said earlier rules out the possibility that concessions of a kind might be worth it from a moral standpoint. The reason, and the trouble, is that moral demands can sometimes come into conflict.

Nothing would be easier than simply setting aside proposals which are somehow morally inadequate, but probably that's just too quick. There is a conceptual untidiness in some honest reflection about the right thing to do, and it can force us to think hard about how we rank our values. Some cases are easier than others. If an axe-murder comes to your door and insists on borrowing your axe, should you lie and say you don't have one? It doesn't take much thinking to come to the conclusion that truthfulness matters, but human lives matter more. Lie away. In these circumstances, it's the right thing to do.

If large parts of the developed world won't agree to action on climate change unless historical emissions are largely ignored, is it right to ignore them? Note that this is not a question about practicality or 'what's realistic', but a moral question about the right thing to do. As we have seen, moral considerations can trump all sorts of economic and practical considerations. What we are worrying about now is whether there is a moral reason for ignoring past inequities. There might turn out to be conflict between two of our criteria: historical responsibility and sustainability. How should we rank them?

There are principles underpinning both, and thinking a little about them can help. Thoughts about historical responsibility depend on such things as the Polluter Pays Principle, as well as the connection between causal and moral responsibility which we paraphrased in Chapter 3 as: 'if you broke it, you bought it'. Thoughts about sustainability are shored up by the value of very many present and a lot more future human lives. This latter value, it seems to me, matters more than moral or causal accountability. It's an awful choice, but if it were the only way to get a firm and meaningful commitment from the world's largest polluters, should we make it?

This line of thinking can lead to the view that our emphasis should be on something other than equal per capita shares of emissions, something which would not place all or almost all of the burdens on the richer nations of the world. Instead, we might consider pushing for something more palatable to the rich: equal marginal costs, comparable burdens, or a fair division of the chores associated with dealing with changes to our climate and altering our energy use.

Traxler sees the problem of climate change as a commons problem, which, as we have seen, is characterized by strong motivations against co-operation to achieve a common goal. The incentive to act selfishly might be reduced, co-operation might become more likely, if everyone sees that everyone else is contributing equally towards a shared end. This can be achieved if the chores required for the end are divvied up fairly. Equally burdensome shares, for Traxler, are defined in terms of opportunity costs. Opportunity costs, he argues, 'measure the difference in returns (to the country in question) of using its resources to deal with climate change rather than of using them in other, presumably more remunerative or beneficial ways. This is the burden a country shoulders: the opportunity for improvement it misses.'[23] So each nation's share of the burdens associated with action on climate change is equally painful for each nation, even though the costs themselves in monetary terms might be quite different.

There are three advantages to this proposal, according to Traxler. First, because the view ignores past injustices, it avoids recrimination and ill will; it therefore stands a solid chance of leading to agreement. Further, he argues that if we were to take account of the histories of emissions and translate those histories into allocations, we'd have to have broad agreement on what constitutes international distributive justice. He doubts 'that such an agreement is likely in our lifetime' and therefore concludes that taking history seriously amounts to putting off action on climate change indefinitely.

If that were true, then we would have a glaring conflict between historical responsibility and sustainability, but as Gardiner points out, persuasively, there's really no reason to think that a complete analysis of international justice is required before negotiations can begin or cuts can be implemented.[24] It is also possible to wonder whether ignoring history is likely to avoid ill will, as Traxler suggests, or lead straight to it. There might be a lot of ill will, most notably in Brazil, if we choose to ignore the past. Some compromise might be required, but why force it in favour of the rich?

Second, Traxler argues that the notion of fair chores can provide a kind of background assumption in favour of fairness as such. It might help weaker nations get a better deal, because everyone can see, from the outset, the unfairness of other bargaining outcomes. However, it almost goes without saying that four other criteria of moral adequacy would do much the same – maybe they'd do better. Certainly they too would provide a framework for securing a fair deal for all. Furthermore, if helping weaker nations matters, if that's partly what recommends fair chores, then the importance of historical emissions matters too, doesn't it?

Third, and most importantly for Traxler and for us, fair chore division gives each nation no stronger reason to defect from the co-operative effort than any other nation. This, he argues, 'would place the most moral pressure possible on each nation to do its part'. If everyone has equally painful burdens to cope with, and everyone can see that everyone else has equally painful burdens, then defection is much less likely than would be the case if, say, the rich were forced to take huge cuts while the poor continued to emit willy-nilly. The policy of fair chore division, Traxler admits, 'remains morally problematic for neglecting past iniquities', but it 'best promotes international co-operation'.

What do you do with that thought? Let's put aside the possibility that Traxler is wrong about fair chores being the best chance for international co-operation and assume for the sake of argument that he's right.[25] Suppose it were true that a morally problematic agreement is the best hope for meaningful action on climate change. You don't need to do too much supposing. It's entirely possible that the US might have signed up to Kyoto if the developing world had agreed to something morally problematic, namely immediate and binding emissions cuts. The powerful nations of the world really did insist on Kyoto targets which had nothing to do with sustainability or responsibility or present capacities. What if it turns out that the only way to achieve international co-operation is to settle for a morally problematic agreement?

As I said before, if there is a conflict between sustainability and the other criteria, in this case historical responsibility, I get the feeling that sustainability wins. I don't have a knock-down argument for this conclusion, but what bothers me is what you get if you deny it. Suppose, instead, that we say that the right thing to do is to hold on to principle, even if it means that we end up with no agreement for meaningful action on climate change. Maybe this stand is admirable, until you think a little about the people who are going to suffer for it, those who come after us and into an unsustainable world, as well as those who are already suffering now and might have some relief through even a problematic deal. You can die for your own principles, if you like, but can you really insist that others die for them, too?

There might be a way out of this, but it's hard to find a way to be happy about it. The reason negotiators might have to settle for less than a morally satisfactory agreement has something to do with worries about defection. Traxler, for example, argues that the problem of allocating the costs associated with climate change is compounded by the fact that there is no policing body, no supra-national authority which might ensure compliance. Fair chore division, he says, 'best promotes international co-operation in the absence of such an overseeing authority'. If governments had to stick to agreements, had to honour obligations, had to recognize moral responsibilities, then maybe we wouldn't have to settle for morally dubious agreements. Perhaps recalcitrant governments can be forced into compliance. If a government does not find moral demands too demanding, then you can end up thinking that Hobbes was right: covenants without the sword are but words. What's needed is force.

Sanctions are one sort of sword sometimes brought up in this connection – there are others, much worse and more problematic, which we'll ignore here. Singer notes that countries have got together in the past, through the mechanisms of the UN, and imposed sanctions on a country precisely because it did or con-tinued to do something unethical.[26] There are trade embargoes, divestments, various forms of cultural boycotting and other, nearby sorts of protest. Singer's example is South Africa under apartheid. Many people agree that sanctions against South Africa were certainly warranted. Given this, the point Singer makes is striking:

> Arguably, the case for sanctions against a nation that is causing harm, often fatal, to the citizens of other countries is even stronger than the case for sanctions against a country like South Africa under apartheid, since that government, iniquitous as its policies were, was not a threat to other countries.

If sanctions against South Africa were deemed appropriate, the case for sanctions against a country which does not face up to its responsibilities with regard to climate change is even greater. South Africa harmed only its own people. A country which ignores the demands of sustainability has a share in the harm of people all over the world, has a share in the droughts and crop failures, the fate of people starving to death right now and in the future. It might not be going too far to suggest that sanctions are not only warranted, but also demanded.

Efforts within a country which behaves unethically, measures undertaken by that country's citizens, are a kind of sword too.

6   Individual Choices

Anybody can become angry. That is easy. But to be angry with the right person and to the right degree and at the right time and for the right purpose, and in the right way – that is not within everybody's power and is not easy.

Aristotle

Most of this book has been about the ethics of climate change and collections of people, namely governments or states or even large corporations. Our focus narrows now to the ethics of climate change and the individual person. There is a lot of talk in the philosophical literature and elsewhere about the moral demands of climate change, but almost none of it has to do with moral demands placed on us just in so far as we are individual people. What you sometimes find, in popular books and other discussions in the public world, is a final chapter or thought which explains 'how you can save the planet', perhaps by recycling or switching to energy-saving bulbs, certainly by minimizing your carbon footprint in various ways. I do think you have a moral obligation to do all of these little things and other, larger things too. I do think your life ought to change, perhaps change radically, depending on the life that you have. But I don't think you can save the planet. We'll get to this unsteady conclusion in due course.

Meanwhile, we need a segue between thoughts about the moral demands placed on governments and thoughts about the moral status of the choices made by individual people. There's an obvious if uncomfortable route, and we'll take it.

CONSISTENCY AGAIN

Many of the world's largest polluters have appalling records when it comes to doing something about climate change. As we have seen, for example, the US is under a great deal of moral pressure to take action, but it has actually done very little if anything to mitigate its emissions or help its own poor or those elsewhere adapt to climate change. Part of the recent response to America's various failures in this connection consists in moral outrage.[1] It is hard to think of this outrage as misplaced or unfounded, but what arguments underpin it? We've thought a little about this already, but it won't hurt to cover some of the ground again briefly if a little more slowly in places.

First, the moral outrage directed towards America has to do with a relation between America's carbon output and its obligation to take action. The USA, with less than 5 per cent of the planet's population, is responsible for the largest share of carbon dioxide emissions by country each year: 24 per cent of global emissions, or 5,872 million metric tons.[2] It's been like this for a while. To give you some idea of just how wildly disproportionate this is, note that China is second on the list, with 14.5 per cent of emissions or 3,300 million metric tons. Do bear in mind, as you reflect on this, that China has about a billion more people in it than the US. The numbers then drop off dramatically, with Russia checking in at 1,432 million metric tons, or about 5.9 per cent of the share of global total carbon emissions.

We've considered the details of the moral demand for action before, but for now just take the following sentence at face value. If America is responsible for the largest share of carbon emissions, and carbon emissions are linked to the adverse effects of climate change, then America has the largest obligation to take immediate action on climate change. The fact that it has done so little about climate change, given its status as the largest polluter, is part of the source of moral outrage.

The second source of moral outrage has to do with what we've called 'present capacities', and depends on the claim that America ought to do something about climate change because it is best placed to do so. There are two aspects to this thought. First, a high percentage of America's emissions, when compared to those of countries in the so-called developing world, are luxury emissions. The US has the room for emissions cuts. Second, America is well placed to do something in certain practical senses as well. America is the world's only Superpower. It has the brains and the economic strength and the resources generally to accomplish a great deal with regard to carbon emissions. Despite all of this, it has done almost nothing to slow or adapt to climate change and quite a bit to exacerbate it.

The third source of moral outrage might well inform voices which become louder and louder if international treaties with more teeth than Kyoto come into being. The objection has to do with some countries taking steps to reduce emissions, and therefore suffering some sort of short-term discomfort or harm, while the US pursues its short-term interests and benefits accordingly.

The line of thinking underpinning this seems not too far from some version of free-rider objections. It can take many forms, all of which are entrenched in our thinking about right and wrong. Maybe it's just the view that getting something while contributing nothing – particularly when others contribute – is wrong. Perhaps it depends on a slightly different principle: the pursuit of self-interest while others pursue the group's interest at some cost to themselves is wrong. It might be something like this: getting something at the expense of the unwitting sacrifice of others is wrong. The wrongness can, if you like, depend on some further conception of fairness or justice, or possibly it has more to do with treating others simply as a means.

Other sources of moral outrage are possible – we are ignoring thoughts about sustainability and ecosystems and other forms of life for the moment – but we have enough now to reach a worrying conclusion. Here's the rub. If you find America's failings morally outrageous, maybe you should find your own failings in the same connection morally outrageous too. Try not to flinch from the thought or take it too personally, if doing so will stop you from taking it seriously. For what it's worth, it's not just you, but me and everyone else living in a high-carbon society.

Morality, as we noted in Chapter 2, insists on a kind of humane consistency. A fair share of remonstration in moral matters amounts to pointing out inconsistencies in an opponent's thinking. If you buy into any of the arguments above, then consistency might demand that you come around to the conclusion that your own behaviour is a kind of moral outrage too.

According to the first line of thinking, we rightly find fault in America's failure to take action on climate change because it is responsible for the largest share of global emissions yet does little about it. In fact, it's likely that your activities result in a hugely disproportionate share of greenhouse-gas emissions when compared to most other individuals on the planet. You can think of this historically or in terms of present emissions if you like. If you live in the US, your yearly activities result in more than 20 metric tons of carbon dioxide on average; Australians contribute 19 metric tons per capita; Canadians emit about 18 metric tons each year; and UK residents are responsible for about 9.5 metric tons. On a list of 211 countries by carbon emissions per capita, US residents come 11th, Australians are 12th, Canadians are 13th, and UK residents are 38th. The people living in the bottom 73 countries, almost half of the countries on the list, emit less than a single metric ton of carbon dioxide each year. Some are responsible for no measurable level of greenhouse gases at all. Your individual emissions are probably massive compared to the many individuals who populate the countries on the bottom half of the list. Maybe you haven't done much about it, haven't taken measures to reduce drastically your carbon output. Not many people have.

The second line of thinking – America ought to take action against climate change because it is best placed to do so – might fit your case too. If you are reading this, you might well be a student or lecturer at some university or other, maybe a graduate of a university, at least a person who reads books with 'ethics' in the title. It seems likely that you have more brains than most people on the planet. If that's too much for you, then at least it's likely that you have been formally educated for much longer than most people. Certainly you have more than enough smarts to research and implement the steps needed to reduce your contribution to climate change. You are smart enough to work out what you should do.

You also probably have much more economic power than the vast majority of people on the planet. You could invest in more efficient appliances, compact fluorescent bulbs, a bike – maybe you've got the cash to install a gas condensing combination boiler or a micro windmill. You might have more free time than someone who farms for her food, and you could take all sorts of action if you chose to do so. Probably you also do not burn fossil fuels primarily for subsistence; you've got lots of luxury emissions which could be cut without much discomfort. Compared to most people on the planet, you are exceptionally well placed to do something about your own greenhouse-gas emissions.

The third line of thinking might fit you too, although I admit it's a tougher case to make. The difficulty lies in the temporal component attached to benefits. The benefits which accrue to tightening belts now might not be visible for some time. Still, if you compare your behaviour to that of some people in the world, people who are making sacrifices to cut emissions while you fail to do so, you might have reason to shift in your chair. If you think about people in the future who will have to cut back a lot because we are not cutting back now, you might shift in your chair a bit more. We are enjoying the benefits of untrammelled energy expenditure while others curb or will curb their own desires for the common good. As noticed a moment ago in the case of the US, I think the strength of this objection as it applies to individuals will become more compelling as more people make serious sacrifices to reduce their carbon footprints.

What do we do with these uncomfortable thoughts? I know as well as you do that individuals are not states, and I have known since I read Plato's *Republic* that it is easy to make mistakes when you compare the two. We are not doing anything like that here. This is not an argument by analogy. It's a call for consistency in our thinking, and that's as legitimate a move in a debate about right and wrong action as you are likely to get. In a nutshell, if you find America's or some other country's behaviour morally outrageous, and the principles operative in your thinking this apply to you too, then you should find your own behaviour morally outrageous as well.

How outrageous? Is overfilling the kettle morally wrong? Is doing nothing about a badly insulated house a kind of evil? Are we making a moral mistake by taking long-haul flights to far-flung holiday destinations? Is it wrong to eat strawberries flown in from abroad? Is a long, hot shower a sin? I have difficulty talking myself into the view that my individual wrongs carry the same weight as the wrongs of America or large companies like Exxon. Probably my difficulty is rooted in the different magnitudes of harm: the harm I do in my everyday life compared to the enormous harm America does in failing to curb its emissions. My effects are smaller.

I worry that the magnitude of the harm is the only relevant difference. A lake full of water and a cup full of water are full of the same stuff. It might be that both my failure and America's failure are the same sort of wrongs, the same in kind, different only in magnitude. It is possible to think that my failure to do something about my high-carbon lifestyle really is morally outrageous. Holding on to the thought isn't easy. Finding a way from it to action is even more difficult.

PSYCHOLOGICAL BARRIERS

By now – having heard a lot about the fact of climate change, the human role in it, and the moral demands associated with all of this – you might wonder why so little has been done. I certainly do not mean to oversimplify by reducing a complex thing to just one or two explanatory principles. We can leave the social or psychological explanation for our collective and individual inaction to others. What's of interest to us, from a philosophical point of view, are arguments, rational justifications, for what we ought to do about climate change. But when you hunker down over a drink and actually talk through climate change with real live people, when you follow debates in the media and elsewhere, what you find are not arguments. What you bump into, again and again, are not reasons advanced for carefully articulated positions, but something closer to psychological defence mechanisms. What you find is denial.

I'm not willing to do more than dip my toe into the literature on such things as denial, dissociation, repression and the like – feel free to pursue it if you find it interesting. It is, however, a fact in some quarters that the human mind is, among other things, fragile. Without reflection, we block out or otherwise ignore facts which might cause us pain, maybe selectively attend to this as against that. In doing all of this, what we are up to is avoiding inner conflict or maybe just the pain of seeing things as they are. One of the conclusions we are avoiding, perhaps above all the others, is a personal conclusion: I ought to change my comfy life.

Hillman works through ten excuses for inaction, and they will all be familiar to anyone who has spent some time thinking about and debating climate change.[3] We'll consider each one, very quickly, with a view towards evaluating it as part of personal arguments for the conclusion that no action on climate change is required. Some of them, you'll notice immediately, seem like nothing more than brute expressions of psychological defence mechanisms. This, anyway, is the charitable interpretation. If they actually were arguments or premises, they would be such bad examples that it is difficult to see how anyone could take them seriously.

1. 'I don't believe in climate change.' Sometimes people latch on, with a sigh of relief, to a single dubious report about sunspots or the fictional work of a popular writer. It is hard to think of these sorts of claims as anything other than simple denial, a refusal to accept established facts.

2. 'Technology will be able to halt climate change.' What we saw as simple wishful thinking in Chapter 4 might really be something else: optimism rooted in a psychological bias against facing up to the painful fact that life has to change. Wishful thinking, we already noted, is not reasoned belief.

3. 'I blame the government or the Americans or the Chinese.' Psychologists talk a lot about projection, a shift of one's own unwanted characteristics on to another person who one can denounce without fear of censure. The fact that others are doing wrong is no reason for inaction on your part, if what you are up to is wrong too.

4. Various *ad hominems* directed against those calling for action. Hillman uses the phrase 'shooting the messenger', but philosophers call this sort of thing an '*ad hominem* argument', a kind of informal fallacy in which 'the man', not his argument, is attacked. There is a kind of pointy-headed anti-environmentalism, which needs to die the death, and is best characterized by drawing attention to some hypocrisy in the life of the person arguing for action on climate change. ('But you wrote that book on *paper*. You killed trees!') These claims about a person might be true, but they have no bearing on the truth or falsity of his conclusions.

5. 'It's not my problem.' This might just be straightforward dissociation, a mechanism by which one distances oneself from a painful conclusion. You often hear people say that they'll be dead by the time climate change is upon us, but of course it already is upon us. It already is our problem.

6. 'There's nothing I can do about it.' Taken in one way, this claim is obviously false. How a person lives a life, how a person uses energy, just is doing something about climate change – maybe contributing to it. However, there are beefier versions of this thought – we considered one of them, the Blair worry, in Chapter 4. We'll come on to other aspects of it when we think about consequences in a moment.

7. 'How I run my life is my business.' This excuse has a number of forms. You might have heard one already: Bush the elder's assertion that 'the American way of life is not up for negotiation'. There are all sorts of lesser claims about artificial necessities in everyday lives, the claim that a person 'can't live' without his mobile phone or 'has to use his car' because public transport is not reliable enough. How a person lives is always up to him, unless how a person lives has bad effects on others. Irresponsible lives of high consumption have consequences beyond the short-term gratification of individual people.

8. 'There are more important and urgent problems to tackle.' This claim might be true, although I'd need to hear an argument for it. It is, anyway, a kind of misdirection. Certainly nothing is stopping us from doing something about more than one of the world's ills.

9. 'At least I am doing something.' You hear this from well-intentioned recyclers and people who tell you they do more than most people about climate change. Certainly it is difficult to feel venomous about this sort of excuse, but in many cases these activities are only marginal or tiny changes in lives, really only efforts at self-consolation or the easing of consciences. Doing something about climate change is probably considerably more demanding than minor life-changes.

10. 'We are already making a lot of progress on climate change.' Inner conflicts can be resolved, sometimes, by focusing on the positive features of a problem and ignoring what would otherwise be glaring difficulties. It's a kind of sleight-of-hand

favoured by some politicians. You might hear an inflated fact or two about cars getting better gas mileage, and this might distract you from the further fact that emissions generally are still on the rise, more roads are being built, and more cars are being driven.

Many of these mechanisms are noticed in a study conducted by Stoll-Kleemann *et al*.[4] They identify a large number of different kinds of denial which muddle our thoughts about action on climate change. We displace or shift our commitments, claiming that we protect the environment in one way while damaging it in another. We deny responsibility and blame by pointing to other, larger causes of climate change. We plead ignorance or anyway avoid thinking about climate change, sometimes reinforcing good thoughts about ourselves by saying that thinking about the destruction of the planet is too painful for us. We claim that we are powerless or that our acts are inconsequential, that whatever we do, we can make no difference at all. We fabricate constraints and impediments, make the task of doing something seem even worse than it might be.

Stoll-Kleemann argues that these barriers are further reinforced by four sorts of general spins, general takes we have on climate change itself. There is a general unwillingness to change certain habits, certain ways of living, particularly if they are tied to an individual's sense of self-identity. Although the authors do not point it out, it seems to me that a lifetime of exposure to a certain sort of advertising which ties who we want to be with what we ought to buy is a part of this spin on refusing to act. There is also a general hope or faith in some sort of managerial or technological quick fix, and this hope is hard to budge. There is a worry that individual action on climate change will involve costs to oneself but benefits only to others – a kind of echo of the tragedy of the commons. Finally, for some at least, there is a general distrust of government, maybe the thought that it will not act as it promises or that it will use climate change to force through taxes or policies it wants for other reasons.

It's important to notice that none of these strategies or mechanisms or spins is an argument. None of them counts as a full-blooded reason, a justification, for our inaction. Given the importance of finding justifications for our moral beliefs, all of this is something to guard against in oneself, to put to one side very quickly, when trying to think clearly about what to do.

INDIVIDUAL ACTION

The call for consistency a few pages back, with respect to the moral outrage one might feel in connection with climate change and governments, might be a kind of argument for action on the part of the individual. It is at least a nudge towards such an argument, perhaps an indication that further reflection on one's own life is required. If such reflection is warranted, how might it go? We can do no more than point towards some answers in the space we have here. We'd need a few books to get through the matter carefully, but there's no harm in at least gesturing in what looks like the right direction. The point now is not to push a conclusion on you, but to point you towards some conclusions about your own life which you might work out for yourself.

Living deliberately, to borrow Thoreau's excellent turn of phrase, is not something most of us do. There's not much wrong with this, of course, and it would be preposterous to suggest that we all attend to our lives as carefully as did Thoreau. It is, anyway, true that we do not think much about how we live, much less about the moral status of our lives as such. Instead, at least some of the time, we go with the flow of life, drift along until we bump into something which calls for a thought or two. Sometimes what we bump into is a moral question or dilemma or problem, a worry about the rightness or wrongness of a particular course of action. Sometimes we stumble into something nearer a crisis, a much larger question about the general way we ought to live, what sort of person we ought to be. These crises about the course or nature of a life really can be primarily moral in flavour, however else they might seem at the time. Reflection on climate change and what to do about it in your own life can feel like something in between a moral problem or question and a crisis – better, it can seem to have some of the properties of both.

The Ancient Greeks and Romans worried more about the whole of a life than particular moral dilemmas. Philosophy itself really got going when its hero, Socrates, went on about the importance of living an examined life, a life which inquires into virtue and lives according to the results. Without knowing something about the nature of virtue, he argues, one really cannot live virtuously. It is, anyway, the virtuous life, the whole of a life and the way it's lived, which interests Socrates and the Ancients. Moral philosophers nowadays are exercised by a number of issues, but as a species they are much more concerned with moral dilemmas or particular questions than the whole of a life.

You won't find many seminars convened this spring on the good life as such, but you will find discussions of smaller moral problems. The discussions get going with questions like these: What should you do if you make conflicting promises? Is euthanasia without consent ever justified? Is abortion as a means of birth control acceptable? Can a terrorist act undertaken to improve lives be considered morally right? Is a pre-emptive war ever just? The list can go on for a while, but for each of these kinds of question the task of the moral philosopher is to find a way through to an answer, and usually the answer is somehow grounded in one of just a few normative ethical theories. There are other views out there, but think again about the two dominant ones: utilitarianism and Kantianism. Probably both views can help with moral crises too.

To remind you, utilitarianism is the view that the rightness or wrongness of an action is determined entirely by its consequences. If its consequences increase human happiness, maximize the overall balance of pleasure over pain, perhaps satisfy the most preferences, then it's the right thing to do. For Kant, what matters are not consequences, but obeying the moral law itself, and the moral status of an action can be teased out by thinking about the universalizability of maxims. Is there anything in here which might help an individual think through climate change? Probably there is a lot of help to be had, but a great deal of care will be needed too. Don't take the following too seriously; it is just a short sketch which might get you started.

A Kantian might be persuaded by the thought that any action described by an environmentally unsustainable maxim, whatever that action might be, almost has to fail to pass muster. For Kant, actions are undertaken under maxims or rules, such as 'don't steal' or 'when I think I need some money, I will borrow it and promise to repay it, though I know I never can do so', or 'never lie'. Kant's test for such maxims is universalizability. Suppose the maxim under consideration were to become a universal law, a maxim adopted automatically by everybody. Would a world with that law be consistent or self-contradictory? If the former, you are in no danger of doing the wrong thing, but if the latter, you are in violation of the moral law. So, for example, if everybody made false promises, no one would believe a promise, so promising itself would be impossible. A world built on false promises ends up undermining itself, turning into a world without any kind of promise-making at all.

Pick an unsustainable maxim: 'consume as much as you can', or 'don't conserve finite resources', or 'use a disproportionate share of a finite good'. It doesn't take much to see that these maxims cannot be universalized. If everyone consumed as much as they could, there would be nothing much left to consume. Consumption on a certain scale undermines consumption itself. If resources weren't conserved, there'd be no resources to use. Finally, not everyone can use a disproportionate share of a finite good – only proportional uses are possible for everyone. The very fact that the maxims are themselves part of an unsustainable order means that they could never be universal laws, never part of consistent worlds, never in keeping with the moral law.

Kantian reflection looks fruitful, looks like the sort of thing which really might help a person think through the choices he might make in the face of climate change.

Utilitarianism is no less promising. Singer argues that a number of principles operative in our thinking about climate change generally might be justified on utilitarian grounds.[5] The Polluter Pays Principle, for example, might be endorsed by a utilitarian who notes that the principle itself sets up a strong incentive to be careful about causing pollution or doing damage to the environment, no doubt to the general benefit of all. A utilitarian might also see the wisdom of greatly favouring the worst-off. If a person already has considerable wealth, then giving him more does not affect his happiness much. Giving the poor even a little more might be a boon, might do a lot to make a life better. These sorts of thoughts could incline an individual to make different choices in a life, maybe vote differently too.

What stands in the way of a great deal of personal utilitarian calculation, though, is the thought we've already had a few times: individual choices cannot possibly matter all that much. The thought might be a part of the reason why it is so hard to take the view that the little things I might do in my life are a kind of moral outrage – for example, the claim that overfilling the kettle or taking a flight for a weekend away are genuine wrongs.

There are many things to say about the thought – we've had a go at examination in Chapter 3 and diagnosis in the previous section – but think now about getting around it. The first thing a consequentialist should notice, against the claim that individual choices cannot matter much, is that nothing else about you stands a chance of making a moral difference at all. If anything matters, it's all those little choices. This rejoinder shows up all over the place, just about anywhere you hear the claim that nothing a single person can do could possibly make a difference. The little effects are the only effects you'll ever have. The only chance you have of making a moral difference consists in the individual choices you make.

The second thing you might try on is a larger conception of you and your effects. Think not about the individual moments, but about the whole of a life, the sum total of the effects which your seemingly insignificant choices have. Compare the total effects of a life of high consumption with a life lived a little closer to the Earth. It's possible to see that your individual choices add up. Lives really do have consequences, even if the whole picture is hard to view clearly from our everyday, limited perspective. This line of thinking can lead to questions about the whole of a life – if not quite a crisis, not a mere moral problem either.

There is a third thought, a kind of frustration. Suppose that you come to the conclusion that your life ought to change, that the choices you make should be different from now on, have less environmentally damaging effects. Given the way our societies are set up, given the fact that we are all enmeshed in a fossil-fuel burning world, it's hard to make better choices. Hypocrisy is where you find it, and you can find it everywhere, in every effort to do what's right. Maybe it's not quite possible to live a life entirely free of morally dubious effects on the planet, at least not for us in the West. Some lives are certainly better than others, but all lives in this kind of world have a share in an unfolding disaster. Having breakfast without doing some sort of damage can seem impossible. Maybe no choice you make on your own can get you entirely clear of moral trouble, much less can you save the planet. This, and no doubt other thoughts too, can lead you to one last conclusion. You can hope to change not just your life, but your society. You can even be drawn to the view that collective action on climate change is not just desirable, but morally required.

CIVIL DISOBEDIENCE

Societies are things which can and do change quite a bit, and sometimes the changes are internally motivated, brought about by collective groups of like-minded people. Collective action can be of many types, but it can help to think broadly of civilly obedient and disobedient action. The former employs lawful means in the hope that a society might take a different course, and the latter employs other sorts of means. Civil disobedience might be characterized as non-violent, non-revolutionary but still unlawful collective action with political ambition. The hope is to appeal morally or emotionally to those in power – both politicians and the majority of voters. It has other characteristics too. Probably some successful examples will occur to you. Is the campaign for action on climate change the sort of cause which might benefit from collective efforts of this kind? We have had obedient objections for a while. Should we now consider something else?

A number of features of the problem suggest that radical action is in order. Certainly there is the matter of injustice, and civil disobedience has, in the past, been a useful tool in raising awareness about and ultimately changing unjust practices and institutions. Civil disobedience is also a tactic employed by those who argue that other avenues have had no relevant effects, or that a government has failed in its duties or otherwise failed to represent its own people. Again, it is possible to see climate change as fitting the bill. There is also a sense of urgency sometimes associated with acts of civil disobedience, the view that some practice simply ought not to continue a moment longer. It is hard to think of action on climate change as anything but urgent.

Other aspects of climate change suggest that it will never be the subject of successful collective action of this kind. As Monbiot puts it, 'nobody ever rioted for austerity'.[6] In more than a token sense, a campaign of civil disobedience undertaken for meaningful action on climate change is nothing other than a campaign by us, against us. Civil disobedience certainly has a history of individuals standing up for their own lives or the improvement of the lives of others, but has anyone anywhere insisted that she be given less? Will we chain ourselves to airplanes and demand more expensive airport taxes? It can seem less than rational.

You can think of it this way, if you like, or you can focus on something else. Collective action on climate change might be the demand for less stuff, but it is also the demand for more of something else: maybe justice or goodness or whatever it is about us which is best. There is nothing irrational about insisting on a more humane world.

Epilogue

The end of a book on climate change can be a dangerous place. Books on the subject have a worrying tendency to veer off into grandeur about five pages from the end. It's entirely forgivable – the subject almost demands it. An uncontrollable urge to engage in some soothsaying just overpowers an author, and odds are that you'll hear a view or two about the likely course of human history against the backdrop of climate change. Philosophers are not much good at prediction, and I certainly won't go in for it. But it is worth noticing the trends which come up in this connection.

A few throw in the towel and conclude that we're doomed. They say that it's too late to make the changes necessary to head off the worst of climate change. Maybe we've crossed some boundaries, blundered past a tipping point or two, perhaps we've already done terminal damage to the planet. But this is just hopelessness, chronic world-weariness, possibly part of a defence mechanism we noticed in the final chapter. Whatever it is, it's not a considered opinion, not rooted in fact or even a view near the mainstream of thinking on climate change. Almost everyone who thinks about the future of our changing world thinks that action can still count. Some go so far as to say that our actions, the choices our generation makes in the next few years, will ripple out into the future and have the kinds of effects no other generation has ever had.

Many more say something remarkable, something uplifting and hopeful. They say that climate change offers humanity the chance to do the right thing. We might be about to cast aside thousands of years of stupidity and finally join together to defeat a common enemy. We have a long history of in-group co-opera-tion for out-group conflict. But what if our changing, inhospitable world makes us see past our superficial differences and finally rec-ognize our common humanity? We are good at joining together in adversity. Maybe the adversity to come will unite us, once and for all.

Still, others sit on an uncomfortable part of the fence. They say, more than a little darkly, that if we screw up our world then maybe we have it coming. There's a slow-motion catastrophe on the cards, and we've seen it coming for a while. We know exactly what we should do about it: we should change our comfortable lives, tighten our belts and cut back on our easy lives of high-energy expenditure. In short, we should make some sacrifices for other people, and we know it. If we do not manage even this, they say, probably our species isn't the noble or wonderful thing we thought it was. If we wipe ourselves out, it's not much of a loss.

I just don't know what to make of such conclusions.

When I started researching this book, I carried a little notebook around and jotted down references to climate change in the national press. Stories started appearing about once a week, then twice a week, then just about daily, and soon I happily put the notebook aside. Somewhere in the summer of 2006, the world suddenly noticed climate change. It made the headlines on a regular basis. Reporters were gamely poking around in the Arctic, filming collapsing icebergs and star-struck polar bears. When I proposed this book to the publisher, I thought an epilogue would be an excellent idea. Things were happening so quickly. It would be good to have a place at the end of the book to bring everything bang up to date. I even thought, with a genuinely warm heart, that maybe the book would be out of date by the time it was written. The world was waking up to climate change. People, many of them without beards, were talking seriously about rainforests, conservation and how best to save energy. Celebrities were making solar panels and hybrid cars sexy. I almost came to the thought that a clutch of arguments about the ethics of climate change weren't really needed. People were coming around to the conclusions on their own. The thinking was a little too quick.

The momentum is still out there, almost everywhere, but it has yet to translate into meaningful action. According to a BBC World Service poll, which surveyed 22,000 people in 21 countries, large majorities of people all over the world know that we must take action.[1] Nearly 80 per cent of respondents believe that human beings are causing climate change. Nine out of ten people on our planet think that action is necessary, and two-thirds of them go further, holding on to the true belief that 'it is necessary to take major steps starting very soon'.

In spite of all of this, world leaders have done nothing morally adequate about climate change in the 20 years since the first warnings of the IPCC and others. There's a case for the conclusion that what some politicians have done is more than inadequate – maybe clear wrongs have been committed, something on a par with deception for financial or political gain, at the cost of countless lives. We've done nothing much about our individual lives either, despite the changing attitudes, even though we have seen climate change in the papers and on our televisions, maybe even in our back yards. It's not all doom and gloom, of course. We've had petitions, climate camps and marches, concerts raising awareness, even some laws are changing. Individual people and individual states and cities have taken impressive action. It's just nothing near enough.

Despite this, despite myself, I am hopeful. I'm not at all sure that our governments or our corporations will do the right thing, but I sometimes surprise myself with the thought that maybe the rest of us will, the worldwide majority now in favour of action on climate change. I have an old friend who I forgive for occasionally sporting a shirt which says 'Eat the Rich' in large bold letters. When I go on a little too much about this or that moral failing on the part of those who ought to do better, he reminds me that the bad guys always fall in the end. We've never had permanent tyranny or perpetual injustice, even though it can seem that way for a time. Human beings eventually do the right thing. He's right of course. But it would be very good, wouldn't it, if we could get a move on this time?

Notes

Introduction

1. IPCC (2001) TAR, 'Synthesis report, summary for policymakers', available at http://www.ipcc.ch.

Chapter 1

1. Unless otherwise indicated, the facts and figures in this section come from the IPCC (2007) AR4, WGI, 'The physical science basis of climate change', summary for policymakers. All of the reports of the IPCC are available at www.ipcc.ch.
2. Temperatures throughout this book are given in degrees Celsius.
3. International Federation of Red Cross and Red Crescent Societies (2001) *World Disasters Report 2001*, International Federation.
4. S. C. Amstrup *et al* (2006) 'Recent observation of intraspecific predation and cannibalism among polar bears in the southern Beaufort Sea', *Polar Biology*, Vol. 29, 11, 2006.
5. The first set of figures was given in the IPCC's TAR. The recent figures are from the 4AR.
6. James M. Inhofe, US Senator and Chairman, Committee on Environment and Public Works, speech made on 28 July 2003.
7. Committee on the Science of Climate Change, National Research Council (2001) *Climate Change Science: An Analysis of Some Key Questions*, Washington: National Academy Press.

8. American Meteorological Society (2003) 'Climate change research: issues for the atmospheric and related sciences', *Bulletin of the American Meteorological Society*, 84.

9. American Geophysical Union (2003) 'Human impacts on climate', available at www.agu.org/sci_soc/policy/climate_change_position.

10. Tom M. L. Wigley *et al.*, Federal Climate Change Science Program (2006) 'Temperature trends in the lower atmosphere', available at www.climatescience.gov.

11. Joint Science Academies (2005), 'Joint science academies' statement: Global response to climate change', available at www.royalsoc.ac.uk.

12. The statement appeared in *Science* on 18 May 2001.

13. As this book goes to press, an internet search indicates that many more bodies have lent support to the findings of the IPCC.

14. For more details on the science of climate change, see John Houghton (2004) *Global Warming: The Complete Briefing*, Cambridge: Cambridge University Press. If you read it, you will know my large debt to Houghton. Unless otherwise indicated, all of the numbers presented in this section and the next section are from his excellent book, itself rooted in the findings of the IPCC.

15. John Tyndall (1870) *Heat, A Mode of Motion*.

16. Roger Revelle and Hans E. Suess (1957) 'Carbon dioxide exchange between atmosphere and ocean and the question of an increase of atmospheric CO2 during the past decades', *Tellus* 9, pp. 18–27.

17. The details in this section come from the IPCC (2007) 4AR, 'The Physical Science Basis'.

18. C. D. Thomas *et al.* (2004) 'Extinction risk from climate change', *Nature*, 427, 145–8.

19. Edward O. Wilson (2003) *The Future of Life*, Vintage.

20. For a vivid description of possible futures, see Mark Lynas (2007) *Six Degrees*, London: Fourth Estate.

21. This was widely reported, notably by Reuters on 22 November 2000.

22. These details are from Houghton (2004) chapter 7.

23. For the facts and figures, see IPCC (2007) 4AR, WGII, 'Impacts, Adaptation and Vulnerability'.

24. See IPCC (2007) 4AR, WGI, 'The Physical Science Basis'.

25. James Lovelock (2006) *The Revenge of Gaia*, London: Penguin Books.

Chapter 2

1. Jeremy Bentham (1996) *Introduction to the Principles of Morals and Legislation*.
2. Aristotle (1996) *Politics*, Book 1, Chapter 8.
3. See Peter Singer (1993) *Practical Ethics*, Cambridge: Cambridge University Press, for a statement of the utilitarian view and John Hacker–Wright (2007) 'Moral Status in Virtue Ethics' *Philosophy* 82; for the view of virtue ethics. Tom Regan (1983) *The Case for Animal Rights*, London: Routledge and Keegan Paul, for the Kantian view. For an excellent overview of the territory and a compelling account of consequentialism in environmental ethics, see Robin Attfield (2003) *Environmental Ethics*, Cambridge: Polity Press.
4. Paul Taylor (1986) *Respect for Nature*, Princeton: Princeton University Press.
5. For the origins of these thoughts, see Aldo Leopold (1949) *A Sand County Almanac*, Oxford: Oxford University Press; for recent work, see, for example, Holmes Rolston III (1994), 'Value in Nature and the Nature of Value' in Robin Attfield (1994) *Philosophy and the Natural Environment*, Cambridge: Cambridge University Press.
6. Bernard Williams, 'Must a concern for the environment be centred on human beings?' in Lori Gruen and Dale Jamieson (eds), *Reflecting on Nature*, Oxford: Oxford University Press, 1994.

Chapter 3

1. Dale Jamieson (2002) 'Ethics, public policy, and global warming', *Morality's Progress*, Clarendon Press: Oxford, pp. 291–2.
2. Ibid., p. 293.
3. Stephen Gardiner, 'A perfect moral storm: climate change, intergenerational ethics, and the problem of corruption' *Environmental Values* 15 (August 2006), 397–413. There is more to Gardiner's account of the features of the problem than the one which follows.
4. For a start, see William Poundstone (1992) *Prisoner's Dilemma*, New York: Doubleday.
5. G. Hardin (1968) 'The tragedy of the commons', *Science* 162, 1243–8

6. Gardiner calls his version the 'Pure Intergenerational Problem', and his discussion (Gardiner 2006) is instructive.

7. For the philosophical end of things, see Michael Grubb (1995) 'Seeking fair weather: ethics and the international debate on climate change', *International Affairs* 71:3, and Jamieson (2002). We'll get on to this in a little more detail in the next chapter.

8. See, for example, John Rawls (1999) *A Theory of Justice*, Cambridge, MA: Harvard University Press and Brian Barry (1989) *Theories of Justice*, Berkeley: University of Berkeley Press.

9. Whether or not, say, the trees in my country count as part of the common carbon sink, as opposed to my country's carbon sink, is a fair question. Probably the oceans don't count as anyone's sink. All of this is relevant – certainly to questions concerning emissions trading – but we can ignore it for now.

10. For data concerning relatively current emissions, see 'Climate data: insights and observations', *Pew Centre Report*, 2004, available at www. pewclimate.org. The following numbers are from the US Department of Energy's Carbon Dioxide Information Analysis Center (CDIAC) for the United Nations Statistics Division, available at www.unstats. un.org.

11. Data concerning cumulative emissions are from Climate Analysis Indicators Tool (CAIT) version 3.0., Washington, DC: World Resources Institute, 2005, available at www.cait.wri.org.

12. Peter Singer (2004) 'One Atmosphere' in his *One World*, London: Yale University Press.

13. Henry Shue (2000) 'Global environment and international inequality', *International Affairs*, 75.3, 535

14. UN (1992) 'The Rio Declaration on Environment and Development', UN Document A/CONF.151/26.

15. Singer (2004), pp. 33–4.

16. Henry Shue (2000), p. 536.

17. See Henry Shue, (1993) 'Subsistence emissions and luxury emissions', *Law and Policy*, 15.1, 39–59.

18. Shue (2000), p. 537.

19. The point about the irrelevance of spatial distance is best made by Peter Singer in 'Famine, affluence and morality', *Philosophy and Public Affairs*, 1972, 1.1, 229–43. For a detailed consideration of concerns for the future, see 'Taking the future seriously' in Attfield (2003).

20. Simone Weil (1956) 'The *Iliad*, or the power of Force', translated by

Mary McCarthy in *Pendle Hill Pamphlet* no. 91, Wallingford, PA: Pendle Hill Press. See David Wiggins (2006) *Ethics: Twelve Lectures on the Philosophy of Morality*, Cambridge, MA: Harvard University Press.

21. There are interesting questions associated with obligations to future people, but I'm going to ignore them for now. See Derek Parfit (1983) 'Energy and further future: the identity problem' in Douglas MacLean and Peter Brown (eds) *Energy and the Future*, Totowa, NJ: Rowman & Littlefield and Tom Mulgan (2006) *Future People,* Oxford: Clarendon Press, for a lot more on this subject.

22. UN (1987) 'Report of the World Commission on Environment and Development', A/RES/42/187.

Chapter 4

1. President G. W. Bush (2001) 'President Bush discusses global climate change', Press Release, 11 June, 2001.

2. The following facts and figures are from the IPCC (2007) 4AR WGI 'The scientific basis', summary for policymakers, as are the definitions of degrees of certainty. All reports of the IPCC are available at www.ipcc.ch.

3. See Stephen Gardiner (2006), 'A core precautionary principle', *The Journal of Political Philosophy* 14.1, 33–60.

4. President Bush (2001).

5. See, for example, Bjorn Lomborg (2001) *The Sceptical Environmentalist*, Cambridge: Cambridge University Press; Lomborg (ed.) (2006) *How to Spend $50 Billion to Make the World a Better Place*, Cambridge: Cambridge University Press; and also W. D. Nordhaus (ed.) (1998) *Economics and Policy Issues in Climate Change*, Washington, DC: Resources for the Future.

6. Nicholas Stern (2007) *The Economics of Climate Change*, Cambridge: Cambridge University Press.

7. IPCC (2007) 4AR, WGII 'Impacts, adaptation, and vulnerability', summary for policymakers.

8. US Government (2006) 'Review of the second order draft of WGIII contribution *Climate Change 2007: Mitigation of Climate Change*'. This was widely reported. See, for example, 'US answer to global warming: smoke and giant space mirrors', *Guardian*, 27 January 2007.

9. The IPCC (2007), 4AR, WGIII, 'Mitigation of climate change', summary for policymakers.

10. Stephen Pacala and Robert Socolow (2004) 'Stabilization wedges: solving the climate problem for the next 50 years with current technologies' *Science* 305, 968–72.

11. These details appear in a talk by Robert Socolow called 'Stabilization wedges: mitigation tools for the next half century', given to the Met Office as part of a conference called, 'Avoiding dangerous climate change: a scientific symposium on stabilization of greenhouse gases, Met Office' on 3 February 2005. The accompanying pessimism is mine.

12. Data concerning emissions per capita are available at the US Department of Energy's Carbon Dioxide Information Analysis Center (CDIAC) for the United Nations Statistics Division, which can be found here: www.unstats.un.org.

13. The worry turns up in lots of places, but numbers are difficult to find. Those given here are from Mark Clayton 'New coal plants bury Kyoto' *The Christian Science Monitor*, 3 December 2004. The original sources cited are the US Energy Information Administration and various industry estimates. I think we can be reasonably sure of the swamping, even if the numbers we have are only goodish guesses.

14. Peter Singer (2004) pp. 44–5.

15. Henry Shue (1994) 'After you: may action by the rich be contingent upon action by the poor?' *Indiana Journal of Global Legal Studies* 1, 353.

Chapter 5

1. All of this is from CarbonTracker, provided by NOAA ESRL, Boulder, Colorado, USA, available at www.cmdl.noaa.gov/carbontracker.

2. IPCC (2007) 4AR, WGI, 'The physical science basis', summary for policymakers. All of the reports of the IPCC are available at www.ipcc.ch.

3. Some proposals specify front-end policies, instead of aiming for specific targets. There's nothing wrong with this in principle, so long as there are good empirical grounds for thinking that the targets will have sustainable effects.

4. Eileen Claussen, President of the Pew Center, advising the US House of Representatives, Committee on Ways and Means, 28 February 2007.

5. From the Global Commons Institute at www.cgi.org.uk. The GCI recognizes the importance of revising targets in line with new information, but says that we'll have to start with some budget.

6. IPCC 4AR, WGIII, 'Mitigation of climate change', summary for policymakers.

7. Mark Lynas (2007) *Six Degrees*, London: Fourth Estate.

8. George Monbiot (2006) *Heat*, London: Penguin Books.

9. This and the other quotations in this section are from the UNFCCC, available at www.unfccc.int.

10. The Pew Centre (2007) 'Analysis of President Bush's climate change plan', available at www.pewclimate.org.

11. For readable if depressing accounts of the Bush administration's and the fossil fuel industry's tactics, see Ross Gelbspan (2004) *Boiling Point*, New York: Basic Books, and Donald Brown (2002) *American Heat: Ethical Problems with the United States' Response to Global Warming*, Lanham: Rowman & Littlefield.

12. Probably we should find a way to ensure that future people are represented too. See Joel Feinberg, 'The Rights of Animals and Unborn Generations' in William Blackstone (ed.) (1974) *Philosophy & Environmental Crisis*, Athens, GA: University of Georgia Press, and Robin Attfield (2003) *Environmental Ethics*, Cambridge: Polity Press, Chapter 4.

13. Useful discussions of this line of thinking can be found in: Stephen Gardiner (2004) 'The global warming tragedy and the dangerous illusion of the Kyoto Protocol' *Ethics and International Affairs* 18; Elizabeth Desombre (2004) 'Global warming: more common than tragic' *Ethics and International Affairs* 18; and Tom Athanasiou and Paul Baer (2002) *Dead Heat*, New York: Seven Stories Press.

14. For an awe-inspiring, concise treatment of more than 40 proposals, see Daniel Bodansky *et al.* (2004) Report for the Pew Center on Global Climate Change, 'International climate efforts beyond 2012: a survey of approaches', available at www.pewclimate.org. For a good philosophical take on many sorts of proposal, see Micahel Grubb (1995) 'Seeking fair weather: ethics and the international debate on climate change' *International Affairs* 71, and Stephen Gardiner (2004) 'Ethics and global climate change' *Ethics* 114. Both have comprehensive bibliographies.

15. I don't know that anyone takes this view seriously, but it is considered here and there. See H. P. Young and A. Wolf (1991) 'Global warming negotiations: does fairness count?' *Brookings Review* 10.2.

16. For example, Benito Müller makes an interesting case for emphasizing procedural fairness. See Müller (1999) 'Justice in global warming negotiations: how to obtain a procedurally fair compromise' Oxford Institute of Energy Studies, EV26.

17. I secretly admire the Brazilian Proposal, with its emphasis on historical responsibility. But its emphasis on history blinds the thing to the importance of other criteria, notably present capacities. On the Brazilian proposal, for example, Japan gets away with a lot just for industrializing late, even though it's wealthy and responsible for lots of emissions now. The text of the proposal is available at www.unfccc.int.

18. Singer (2002) p. 35.

19. For a good discussion, see Grubb (1995).

20. Shue makes a case for the claim that people have inalienable rights to minimal emissions required for survival. See Shue (1993) 'Subsistence emissions and luxury emissions', *Law and Policy* 15, 39–59. On bad nights you can wonder what to do if it turns out that there are not enough subsistence emissions to go around.

21. John Rawls (1999) *A Theory of Justice*, Cambridge, MA: Harvard University Press.

22. See Aubrey Meyer (2001) *Contraction and Convergence*, Totnes: Green Books, and the various reports and proposals of the Global Commons Institute available at www.gci.org.uk.

23. Martino Traxler (2002) 'Fair chore division for climate change' *Social Theory and Practice* 28.1.

24. Gardiner (2004) p. 583.

25. For good arguments against the claim that Traxler's version supplies the best chance of co-operation, see Gardiner (2004).

26. Singer (2002) p. 50.

Chapter 6

1. Most accounts of the appalling record and expressions of anger appear in newspaper articles, but some recent books express it too. For a start, see Ross Gelbspan (2005) *Boiling Point*, New York: Basic

Books and (1998) *The Heat is On*, Reading, MA: Perseus Books; George Monbiot (2006) *Heat*, London: Penguin Books; and in more measured tones, Elizabeth Kolbert (2006) *Field Notes From A Catastrophe*, New York: Bloomsbury.

2. All figures in this section are from the United Nations Statistics Division, available at www.unstats.un.org.

3. Mayer Hillman (2004) *How We Can Save the Planet*. London: Penguin Books, pp. 54–62.

4. S. Stoll-Kleeman, Tim O'Riordan, and Carlo C. Jaeger (2001) 'The psychology of denial concerning climate mitigation measures: evidence from Swiss focus groups' *Global Environmental Change* 11, pp. 107–17. There is a good discussion of this in Lynas (2007) *Six Degrees*, London: Fourth Estate, pp. 282–8.

5. Singer (2002) pp. 40–3.

6. Monbiot (2006) p. 42.

Epilogue

1. The survey was conducted by the polling firm Globescan and the Program on International Policy Attitudes (Pipa) at the University of Maryland. It was reported widely by the BBC on 25 September 2007.

Bibliography

American Geophysical Union (2003) 'Human impacts on climate', available at www.agu.org/sci_soc/policy/climate_change_position.

American Meteorological Society (2003) 'Climate change research: issues for the atmospheric and related sciences', *Bulletin of the American Meteorological Society*, 84.

Amstrup, S. C. *et al.* (2006) 'Recent observation of intraspecific predation and cannibalism among polar bears in the southern Beaufort Sea', *Polar Biology*, 29.11, 997–1002.

Aristotle, (1996) S. Everson (trans.) *The Politics and the Constitution of Athens*. Cambridge: Cambridge University Press.

Athanasiou, T. and Baer, P. (2002) *Dead Heat*, New York: Seven Stories Press.

Attfield, R. (1991a) *The Ethics of Environmental Concern*, Athens, GA: University of Georgia Press.

— (1991b) *The Ethics of the Global Environment*, Edinburgh: Edinburgh University Press.

— (2003) *Environmental Ethics: An Overview for the Twenty-First Century*, Polity Press: Cambridge.

Barry, B. (1989) *Theories of Justice*, Berkeley: University of Berkeley Press.

Bentham, J. (1996) (J. H. Burns and H. L. A. Hart, eds) *An Introduction to the Principles of Morals and Legislation*, Oxford: Oxford University Press.

Blackstone, W. (ed.) (1974) *Philosophy and Environmental Crisis*, Athens, GA: University of Georgia Press.

Brown, D. (2002) *American Heat: Ethical Problems with the United States' Response to Global Warming*, Lanham: Rowman & Littlefield.

Desombre, E. (2004) 'Global warming: more common than tragic', *Ethics and International Affairs* 18(1), 41–6.

Feinberg, J. (1974) 'The rights of animals and unborn generations' in W. Blackstone (ed.) *Philosophy and Environmental Crisis*, Athens, GA: University of Georgia Press.

Gardiner, S. (2001) 'The real tragedy of the commons', *Philosophy and Public Affairs*, 30.4, 387–416.

— (2003), 'The pure intergenerational problem', *The Monist*, 86.3, 481–500.

— (2004a) 'Ethics and global climate change', *Ethics* 114. 555–600.

— (2004b) 'The global warming tragedy and the dangerous illusion of the Kyoto Protocol', *Ethics and International Affairs* 18.1, 23–39.

— (2006a), 'A Core Precautionary Principle', *The Journal of Political Philosophy* 14.1, 33–60.

— (2006b) 'A perfect moral storm: climate change, intergenerational ethics and the problem of moral corruption', *Environmental Values* 15, 397–413.

Gelbspan, R. (1998) *The Heat is On*, Reading, MA: Perseus Books.

— (2005) *Boiling Point*, New York: Basic Books.

Grubb, M. (1995) 'Seeking fair weather: ethics and the international debate on climate change', *International Affairs* 71.3, 463–96.

Hacker-Wright, J. (2007) 'Moral Status in Virtue Ethics' *Philosophy*, 82.2.

Hardin, G. (1968) 'The tragedy of the commons', *Science* 162, 1243–8.

Hillman, M. (2004) *How We Can Save the Planet*, London: Penguin Books.

Houghton, J. (2004) *Global Warming: The Complete Briefing*, Cambridge: Cambridge University Press.

International Federation of Red Cross and Red Crescent Societies (2001) *World Disasters Report 2001*, International Federation.

IPCC (2001) *Third Assessment Report: Climate Change 2001*, available at http://www.ipcc.ch/pub/reports.

IPCC (2007) *Fourth Assessment Report: Climate Change 2007*, available at http://www.ipcc.ch/pub/reports.

Jamieson, D. (1990) 'Managing the future: public policy, scientific uncertainty, and global warming' in D. Scherer (ed.) *Upstream/Downstream: Essays in Environmental Ethics*, Philadelphia: Temple University Press.

— (1996a) 'Ethics and international climate change', *Climatic Change* 33, 323–36.

— (1996b) 'The epistemology of climate change: some morals for managers', *Society and Natural Resources* 4, 319–29.

— (1996c) 'Scientific uncertainty and the political process', *Annals of the American Academy of Political and Social Science*, 545, 35–43.

Jamieson, D. (1998) 'Global responsibilities: ethics, public health and global environmental change', *Indiana Journal of Global Legal Studies* 5, 99–119.

— (ed.) (2001a) *A Companion to Environmental Philosophy*, Oxford: Blackwell.

— (2001b) 'Climate change and global environmental justice' in P. Edwards and C. Miller (eds), *Changing the Atmosphere: Expert Knowledge and Global Environmental Governance*, Cambridge: MIT Press.

— (2002) *Morality's Progress: Essays on Humans, Other Animals, and the Rest of Nature*, Clarendon Press: Oxford.

Joint Science Academies (2005), 'Joint Science Academies' statement: global response to climate change', available at www.royalsoc.ac.uk.

Kolbert, E. (2006) *Field Notes From A Catastrophe*, New York: Bloomsbury.

Lomborg, B. (2001) *The Sceptical Environmentalist*, Cambridge: Cambridge University Press.

Lomborg, B. (ed.) (2006) *How to Spend $50 Billion to Make the World a Better Place*, Cambridge: Cambridge University Press.

Lovelock, J. (2000) *The Ages of Gaia*, Oxford, Oxford University Press.

— (2006) *The Revenge of Gaia*, London: Penguin Books.

Lynas, M. (2007) *Six Degrees*, London: Fourth Estate.

MacLean, D. and Brown, P. (eds) (1983) *Energy and the Future*, Totowa, NJ: Rowman & Littlefield.

Meyer, A. (2001) *Contraction and Convergence*, Totnes: Green Books.

Monbiot, G. (2006) *Heat*, London: Penguin Books.

Mulgan, T. (2006) *Future People*, Oxford: Clarendon Press.

Müller, B. (1999) 'Justice in global warming negotiations: how to obtain a procedurally fair compromise', Oxford Institute of Energy Studies, EV26.

National Research Council, Committee on the Science of Climate Change, (2001) *Climate Change Science: An Analysis of Some Key Questions*, Washington: National Academy Press.

Nordhaus, W. D. (ed.) (1998) *Economics and Policy Issues in Climate Change*, Washington: Resources for the Future.

Pacala, S. and Socolow, R. (2004) 'Stabilization wedges: solving the climate problem for the next 50 years with current technologies', *Science* 305, 968–72.

Parfit, D. (1983) 'Energy and further future: the identity problem' in D. MacLean and P. Brown (eds) *Energy and the Future*, Totowa, NJ: Rowman & Littlefield.

Poundstone, W. (1992) *Prisoner's Dilemma*, New York: Doubleday.

Rawls, J. (1999) *A Theory of Justice*, Cambridge, MA: Harvard University Press.

Regan, T. (1983) *The Case for Animal Rights*, London: Routledge and Keegan Paul.

Revelle, R. and Suess, H. E. (1957) 'Carbon dioxide exchange between atmosphere and ocean and the question of an increase of atmospheric CO_2 during the past decades', *Tellus* 9, 18–27.

Scherer, D. (ed.) (1990) *Upstream/Downstream: Essays in Environmental Ethics*, Philadelphia: Temple University Press.

Shue, Henry (1992) 'The unavoidability of justice' in A. Hurrell and B. Kingsbury (eds) *The International Politics of the Environment: Actors, Interests, and Institutions*, Oxford: Oxford University Press.

— (1993) 'Subsistence emissions and luxury emissions', *Law and Policy* 15, 39–59.

— (1994) 'After you: may action by the rich be contingent upon action by the poor?', *Indiana Journal of Global Legal Studies* 1, 343–66.

— (1995) 'Ethics, the environment and the changing international order', *International Affairs* 71, 453–61.

— (1996) *Basic Rights: Subsistence, Affluence, and U.S. Foreign Policy*. Princeton: Princeton University Press.

— (2000) 'Global environment and international inequality', *International Affairs*, 75.3, 531–45.

— (2001) 'Climate', in D. Jamieson (ed.) *A Companion to Environmental Philosophy*, Oxford: Blackwell.

Singer, P. (1972) 'Famine, affluence and morality', *Philosophy and Public Affairs*, 1.1, 229–43.

— (1993) *Practical Ethics*, Cambridge: Cambridge University Press.

— (2004) *One World*, London: Yale University Press.

Socolow, R. (2005) 'Stabilization wedges: mitigation tools for the next half century', talk delivered to *Avoiding Dangerous Climate Change: A Scientific Symposium on Stabilization of Greenhouse Gases*, Met Office.

Stern, N. (2007) *The Economics of Climate Change*, Cambridge: Cambridge University Press.

Stoll-Kleeman, S.; O'Riordan, T.; Jaeger, C. C. (2001) 'The psychology of denial concerning climate mitigation measures: evidence from Swiss focus groups', *Global Environmental Change* 11, 107–17.

Taylor, P. (1986) *Respect for Nature*, Princeton: Princeton University Press.

Thomas, C. D. *et al.* (2004) 'Extinction risk from climate change', *Nature*, 427, 145–8.

Traxler, M. (2002) 'Fair chore division for climate change', *Social Theory and Practice* 28.1, 101–34.

Tyndall, J. [1870] (2001) *Heat, A Mode of Motion*, London: Longmans, Green & Co.

UN (1987) 'Report of the World Commission on Environment and Development', A/RES/42/187.

UN (1992) 'The Rio Declaration on Environment and Development', A/CONF.151/26.

Weil, S. (1956) 'The *Iliad*, or the power of force', translated by M. McCarthy in *Pendle Hill Pamphlet* no. 91, Wallingford, PA: Pendle Hill Press.

Wilson, E. O. (2003) *The Future of Life*, New York: Vintage.

Wiggins, D. (2006) *Ethics: Twelve Lectures on the Philosophy of Morality*, Cambidge, MA: Harvard University Press.

Young, H. P. and Wolf, A. (1991) 'Global warming negotiations: does fairness count?', *Brookings Review* 10.2, 46–51.

Index

action, collective 151–3
adequacy, moral 114–19,
        120–35
ages, ice 17–18, 24
Amazon 29
animals, moral concern for 50–4
Antarctica 8, 29, 100
apartheid 134
Aristotle 52, 137, 161
Arrhenius, S. 18–19
Attfield, R. 161, 162, 165
Australia 122

balloons 102
Bangladesh 27, 74, 92
bears, polar 10, 26
bedrock, moral 42–3, 75
Bentham, J. 46, 161
biocentrism 53
biofuels 105–6
Blair, T. 107, 145
bleaching, coral 11
Brown, D. 165
Brundtland 85
burdens, comparable 130–5
Bush, G. 145
Bush, G. W. 90–1, 97–8, 162
business-as-usual 28

Callendar, G. 8, 18–19

capacities, present 3, 76–83,
        114–15, 128, 139
capture, carbon 105
carbon 10, 20 , 104
carbon dioxide 18, 20, 24, 31, 103,
        110, 111, 115, 117 see also
        gasses, greenhouse
cars 105
Carteret Islands 8–9
China 69, 70, 92, 107–8, 138
chores, fair division of 131–5
circulation, ocean thermohaline
        29, 92
climatologists 2, 8
codes, moral 37
commons, tragedy of 60–6, 131,
        146 see also dilemma,
        prisoner's
complexities, spatial and temporal
        59–61
consensus, scientific 7, 13–17
consistency 44–5, 138–42, 154
Contraction and Convergence 129
        -30
cooperation, intergenerational
        59–61, 64, 78–9
cores, ice 21
costs 90, 97–101 see also
        uncertainty
        adaptation 81–2, 115

costs (*cont.*)
   mitigation 81–2, 115, 127
   opportunity 131–5
criteria, moral 114–19, 120–35
Cross, Red 9
cuts, emissions 89, 117, *see also*
   targets

denial 143–7
Descartes, R. 52
Descombre, E. 165
dilemma, prisoner's 61–6 *see also*
   commons, tragedy of
disagreements, moral vs. factual
   44 -5
disease 59, 91
disobedience, civil 131–5
drought 11, 91

Earth Summit 97, *see also* Rio
   Declaration
economics 65, 98, 97–101, *see also*
   costs, uncertainty
effect, greenhouse 19–21, 91, *see*
   also carbon dioxide; gasses,
   greenhouse
El Niño 10–1
emissions *see also* carbon dioxide;
   gasses, greenhouse
  cumulative 69, 90, 107, 115, 127
  cuts 89, 117
  luxury 81, 139, 141
  per capita 69, 107, 126, 140
  subsistence 81, 122, 127–8, 141
  targets 74, 115–17, 120, 121,
   129
emotion 1, 48–9
entitlements 3, 76–83, 15, 128
epistemology 34, 59
equality 67–70, *see also*
   entitlements, fairness, justice
ethics, environmental 3, 34, 49–55
European Union 69, 121, 126

evolution 37
expansion, thermal 8
extinction
  mass 26
  human 30, 156

fairness 80, 108 *see also* chores, fair
   division of; equality; justice,
   procedural 115, 118 *see also*
   criteria, moral
feedback 23, 24, 29, 117
floods 11
footprint, carbon 137, 142
forecasts, weather 21–2
Fourier, J. 17
  fuels, fossil 18, 20, 28, 58, 80, 86,
   91, 107 *see also* carbon
   dioxide; emissions; gasses,
   greenhouse

Gaia 30
Gardiner, S. 4, 59–61, 132, 161,
   162, 165, 166
gasses, greenhouse 15, 17, 23, 58,
   64, 68–9, 98, 108, 112–13,
   115, 126 *see also* carbon
   dioxide; effect, greenhouse;
   emissions; fuels, fossil
Gelbspan, R. 165, 166
genes 37, 40
geo-engineering 102–3
glaciers 8, 9, 26
God 39
gorillas 11, 26
Greenland 8, 26, 29, 92–3
growth, population 128
Grubb, M. 162, 165
Gruen, L 161
Gulf Stream 29, 32, 92–3

Hacker-Wright, J. 161
Hardin, G. 161
Hemmingway, E. 26

Hillman, M. 143–6
Hobbes, T. 134
Högbom, A. 18–19
Houghton, J. 160
Hume, D. 48–9, 84
hurricanes 25, 91
hydrogen 105–6
hypocrisy 110, 144, 151

ice ages 17–18, 24
imperative, categorical 47, see also
    Kant, universalizability
India 70, 107–8
ineptitude, theoretical 59–61
inertia, climactic 60
Inhofe, J. 13, 159
Institute, Global Commons 117,
    129
intuition, moral 49
IPCC 1, 4, 14–16, 23–4, 31, 11,
    91–3, 99–100, 103, 113, 117,
    159–60, 163–4
Islands, Carteret 8–9

Jamieson, D. 4, 58–9, 161
justice 42, see also equality,
    fairness, responsibility
    corrective 67–8, 74
    distributive 66–7, 115, 132
    historical conceptions of 3,
        66–7, 127
    ordinary conception of 126
justification
    moral 2, 33, 35–46
    rational 36

Kant, I. 47–8, 52, 54, 83, 148–50,
    see also imperative,
    categorical; universalizability
Kolbert, E. 166
Kyoto Protocol 3, 64, 90, 97, 99,
    107–8, 110, 119–26, 130, 133,
    139

liability 78
level, sea 8, 15, 27, 59, 73
life, meaning of 39–40
Locke, J. 70–1
Lomborg, B. 98–9, 162
losses, economic 11, see also costs
Lovelock, J. 30, 160
Lynas, M. 117, 160, 164, 167

means and ends 124
Mechanism, Clean Development
    121
mechanisms
    feedback 10, 23–4, 29, 117 see
        also point, tipping
    psychological 143–7
melting, 15
methane 20, 117
Meyer, A. 166
models, climate 21–4
Monbiot, G. 117, 152, 164, 166,
    167
monsoon 25
morality, origins of 37–8
Müller, B. 166

National Academy of Sciences 15
nations
    developed 89, 115–16, 130
    developed and developing 70,
        86, 119
    developing 89, 133
    high income and low income 70
Nietzsche, F. 37
Nordhaus, W. 162

objection, free-rider 139
oceans 8, 18, 93
outrage, moral 138–42

Pacala 103–6, 163
paleoclimatology 24
panels, solar 104–5, 106

Parfit, D. 162
pay, ability to 81–3
permafrost 10, 26, 117
philosophy 34
    applied 4
    moral 3, 33–55
Plato 33, 37, 66, 142
point, tipping 155 *see also*
    mechanisms, feedback
Poundstone, W. 161
principle, greatest happiness 46,
    54 *see also* utilitarianism
principle, no harm 96
Principle, Polluter Pays 74–5, 115,
    150
principle, precautionary 96–7,
    119
problem, intergenerational 59–61,
    78–9
Projects, Joint Implementation
    121
prospects, planetary 7, 24–31
Protocol, Kyoto 3, 64, 90, 97, 99,
    107–8, 110, 119–26, 130, 133,
    139
proximity 84
psychology, social 37, 143
Pythagoras 13

Rawls, J. 128–9, 162, 166
reason 36
recklessness, moral 41, 103,
    110–12
Red Cross 9
reduction, room for 81–3
refugee, climate / environmental
    9, 93
Regan, T. 161
Report, Brundtland 85
responsibility 3
    causal 51, 75–6, 115
    moral 59–87, 115
    historical 114–15, 127, 131

    legal 76, 78
    individual and collective 3, 62–6
Revelle, R. 19, 160
Review, Stern 99–100
Revolution, Industrial 20, 68
Rio Declaration 74–5, 97 *see also*
    Earth Summit
risk 1, 95, 118, 123, 129
Rolston H. 161
Royal Society 16
rum 67–8
Russia 69, 121–2

sanctions 134
scepticism, climate-change 13
Sciences, National Academy of
    15
sea level 8, 15, 27, 59, 73
sea-ice 9
Seneca 89
sensitivity, climate 116
shares, equal per capita 126–30
Shue, H. 4, 72, 79, 82, 109, 162,
    164, 166
Singer, P. 4, 70–3, 75, 108–9 126–8,
    130, 134, 150, 161
sinks, carbon 69, 71–3, 115, 89, 93,
    109, *see also* carbon dioxide;
    effect, greenhouse; gasses,
    greenhouse
Smith, A. 72
Society, American Meteorological
    16, 160
Society, Royal 16
Socolow, R. 103, 6, 164
Socrates 148
stabilization 103–6
status quo 125
Stern Review 99–100
Stern, N. 162
stewardship 85
Stoll-Kleeman 5, 146–7, 167
storage, carbon 105

storylines 31
Suess, H. 18, 160
Summit, Earth 97, see also Rio
    Declaration
sunspots 31
sustainability 2, 3, 31, 83–7,
    114–15, 118, 120–6, 137, 149,
    162, 164, 166–7, see also
    criteria, moral

targets 74, 115–17, 120, 121, 129
    see also cuts, emissions
Taylor, P. 161
technology 31, 101–6, 144
temperature 8, 15, 23, 27
terraforming 102
Thoreau, H. 147
trading, emissions 121–2
Traxler, M. 131–5, 166
Tuvalu 9
Tyndall, J. 7, 17, 19, 160
typhoons 91

uncertainty 7, 12, 90–7, see also
    costs; consensus, scientific
UNFCC 3, 119–26
Union, American Geophysical 16,
    160
Union, European 69, 121, 126

United States 69, 70, 122
universalizability 48, 54, 149 see
    also Kant, I.
urgency 110–12, 152
use, land 20, 91, 105
utilitarianism 46–7, 54, 109–10,
    125, 148–50, see also
    Bentham, J.; principle,
    greatest happiness

value 2
    intrinsic vs instrumental 51–2
variation, natural 13
viciousness 41, 97, 110–12
volcanoes 18, 23, 102
Voltaire 57
Vonnegut, K. 38–9

war 9
Wilson, E. O. 26, 160
Williams, B. 53, 161
Weil, S. 84, 162
wishful thinking 103
windmills 104–6
    waiting 106–10
World Meteorological Association
    14, 27

yurts 60